FROM THE PORCH

Lady Ritchie at the Porch
From a photograph taken by M.rs Cameron at Freshwater

FROM THE PORCH

BY
LADY RITCHIE
(Anne Isabella Thackeray Ritchie)

WITH ILLUSTRATIONS

Essay Index Reprint Series

 BOOKS FOR LIBRARIES PRESS
FREEPORT, NEW YORK

Framingham State College
Framingham, Massachusetts

First Published 1913
Reprinted 1971

INTERNATIONAL STANDARD BOOK NUMBER:
0-8369-2252-2

LIBRARY OF CONGRESS CATALOG CARD NUMBER:
70-152208

PRINTED IN THE UNITED STATES OF AMERICA

DEDICATED

TO OUR FRIEND

RHODA BROUGHTON

October 1913

CONTENTS

DIVAGATIONS

	PAGE
A Discourse on Modern Sibyls	3
Charles Dickens as I remember Him	31
A Dream of Kensington Gardens	46

MONOGRAPHS

Sainte Jeanne Françoise de Chantal	61
Quills from the Swan of Lichfield	84
Mrs. John Taylor, of Norwich	135
L'Art d'être Grandpère	172
Morland at Freshwater Bay	198
Alfred Stevens	208

REMINISCENCES

Concerning the Founding of the "Cornhill Magazine"	227
A Meeting in a Garden	237
Upstairs and Downstairs	244
In My Lady's Chamber	256

ILLUSTRATIONS

Portrait of Lady Ritchie at the Porch . *Frontispiece*

The Porch . . . . . *To face page* 264

DIVAGATIONS

A DISCOURSE ON MODERN SIBYLS[1]

It is not only to unite teachers and to improve teaching that the English Association exists, but also to give in some measure a personal expression to our love of books, to the thoughts and impulses which come from their infinite combinations.

Everything is to be found in book-lore; not only is the generous feast spread out for favoured guests, but the crumbs are there falling from the high tables. There is fun, there is fancy and good-humour, there is companionship for the solitary, comfort for the sad, knowledge of life for the young, and for the elders pleasant gossip and remembrance. Professor Ker has brought Romance before us; Professor Bradley has spoken of Poetry and its uses—who that was present on that last occasion when he spoke will not remember

[1] The Presidential Address delivered at the Annual General Meeting of the English Association, on January 10, 1913. It was read by Mr. Ernest von Glehn.

it? The foggy gloom of the streets invaded the crowded, attentive room, but it was of light, and lovely things, the lecturer discoursed. The wide suggestions appealed to those who could follow them, as well as to those among us who could not always follow with full comprehension, but who appreciated and breathed for the moment with some deeper breath; "living," as Professor Bradley said, "a section of each poet's own life" in the passing realisation of his thought. It may seem presumptuous indeed for a "wren with little quill" to follow such discourses with mere personalities, small in comparison to those larger philosophies, yet a literary association is intended to emphasize and give voice to the various units which compose the whole, as letters are part of a word, words form the sentence, and finally the book of life itself is spread open.

There is no doubt but that different chapters of Literature commend themselves to different generations. A well-known critic, an American lady, Miss Fanny Repplier, also taking a personal standpoint, deplores the misfortune of having been herself born quite a century too late for Success! She appeals to *Evelina*, that work admired by Johnson and Burke; she points to Hannah More, whose tragedies drew tears and praise from Garrick, whose tracts reached Moscow and made their edifying way to Iceland itself. Tracts, such as *Charles the Footman* and the *Shepherd of Salisbury Plain*, are also said to have been found by a missionary in the library of the Rajah of Tanjore. "Those were the days to live in," cries Miss Repplier, "when families tore the *Mysteries of Udolpho* to pieces in their eager interest, when the astounding Miss Seward dazzled the literary world; and unfortunates, born a hundred years too late, may look back with wistful eyes upon an age which they feel themselves qualified to have adorned!"

Some time ago, borrowing a title from a well-known Elizabethan collection of histories, I wrote a little volume called *A Book of Sibyls*. It did not concern classical beings, with flying robes and tripods, uttering incoherent rhymes and oracles at Delphi and elsewhere, but it related to certain women leading notable lives in mobcaps and hobble-skirts. Jane Austen, then as now, was supreme among them, although some sapient critics of her own time considered her "commonplace," and not to compare to the Edgeworths, Barbaulds, and Opies of the day.

When it was first suggested that I should speak to the English Association of yet another generation of Sibyls nearer to my own experience, I could but feel, unlike Miss Repplier, that I had been fortunate indeed in the time of my birth. I do not know whether others will agree with a friend of mine who declares that people reach their complement at from ten to twelve years old, and that they never really change after that time, though they may learn more and more facts. As the years go by, and, alas, the hour for *forgetting* may begin, the same observer still exists throughout the different stages. Mrs. Gaskell and Mrs. Oliphant were my torch-bearers in youth as afterwards. The Brontës were magicians, flashing romance into the little Kensington street in which we dwelt. George Eliot followed. I do not here attempt to speak of all the great masters of the craft then living, but of certain women with whom I have had the privilege of being in some relation. These ladies were dressed not in flying draperies nor in mob-caps and hobble-skirts, but in crinolines—though it seems almost desecration to mention the fact, or to suggest that George Eliot ever wore one. They put on lop-eared bonnets when they went abroad; their parasols were the size of half-crowns; they had sandalled shoes, or odd flat elastic brodequins. Whatever their dress may have been in 1850, they were true Sibyls nevertheless. Their voices were direct and outspoken, they went straight to the heart of things. When I made their acquaintance, I myself was about twelve years old and forbidden by my governess to read novels. No objection was made to the works of Miss Yonge, personally unknown to me indeed, but nevertheless a sympathetic confidante and playfellow. I was older before Miss Braddon wove the spells which my father and Dickens both so warmly praised. My father liked *Lady Audley's Secret;* Dickens specially cared for the story of *The Doctor's Wife.* Many other Sibyls were yet to be, but in those early days they concerned me not. Rhoda Broughton was in her schoolroom, Emily Lawless was in her nursery, Mrs. Humphry Ward in her cradle. Mary Cholmondeley and Margaret Woods were not even born; not to speak of how many others besides, happily yet to be; poets, historians, essayists, whose names will come to all our minds.

My governess herself gave me Mrs. Oliphant's first book as an exception to the rigid rule against novel-reading, saying she heard it had been written by a girl only a few years older than I was. It was in Scotch, which I could not understand, but it was a novel all the same. As to the stern edict of limitation, fortunately for me *Blackwood* was not a novel, but a soberlooking magazine with a brown-paper cover and a picture of George Buchanan, surrounded by thistles; and there it was that a few years later I found the *Scenes from Clerical Life*, all-absorbing, convincing, written as I imagined by one of the wisest of men. I used to try to picture him to myself, grave and noble, with a melancholy reserved manner, rather bald—certainly a clergyman from Cambridge. It was like going to his church to read of Amos and Milly Barton and the people out of *Janet's Repentance* and *Mr. Gilfil's Love Story*, who seemed to fill our house where such good company was already to be found.

There are certain Overtures, like that one to the *Freischütz*, which in the opening bars bring before us all the coming wonder of the great music yet to be. In the same way, it seems now, looking back, that when I wondered over the first opening chapters of George Eliot's work, all the suggestion of its future came flooding in. I cannot think that she has ever given us anything more beautiful than the *Scenes from Clerical Life*, as they dawned then, complete, full of heart and of knowledge — knowledge of that special phase of life which was in her own experience.

The very first sentences of *Amos Barton* open in old Shepperton Church, where George Eliot, as a child herself, is waiting in her place:

"As the moment of psalmody approached, by some process to me as mysterious and untraceable as the opening of the flowers or the breaking-out of the stars, a slate appeared in front of the gallery, advertising in bold characters the psalm about to be sung." Then follows the description of its accompaniment, "the bassoon, the two key-bugles, the carpenter understood to have an amazing power of singing 'counter' who formed the complement of the choir regarded in Shepperton as one of distinguished attraction, occasionally known to draw hearers from the next parish. . . . The greater triumphs were reserved for the Sundays when the slate announced an *Anthem* . . . when the key-bugles always ran away at a great pace, while the bassoon every now and then boomed a flying shot after them. . . ."

Better even than the account of the choir is the noble sermon the author speaks in conclusion, and of which this is the text:

"Blessed influence of one true loving human soul on another! Not calculable by algebra, not deducible by logic, but mysterious, effectual, mighty as the hidden process by which the tiny seed is quickened, and bursts forth into tall stem and broad leaf, and glowing tasseled flower. Ideas are often poor ghosts; our sun-filled eyes cannot discern them; they pass athwart us in thin vapour, and cannot make themselves felt. *But sometimes they are made flesh; they breathe upon us with warm breath, they touch us with soft responsive hands, they look at us with sad sincere eyes,* and speak to us in appealing tones; they are clothed in a living human soul, with all its conflicts, its faith and its love. *Then* their presence is a power, then they shake us like a passion, and we are drawn after them with gentle compulsion, as flame is drawn to flame."

Some one asked me once if I liked books or people best. It is an impossible question to answer. Books *are* people, if they are worth anything at all; just as people at times become books, and are often all the better for the transmigration.

I once had a talk with George Eliot. It was in winter time with the snow lying on the ground. She sat by the fire in a beautiful black satin gown, with a green-shaded lamp on the table beside her, where I saw German books lying and pamphlets and ivory paper-cutters. She was very quiet and noble, with two steady little eyes and a sweet voice. As I looked I felt her to be a friend, not exactly a personal friend but a good and benevolent impulse. I remember she said "it was better in life to build one's cottage in a valley so as to face the worst and not to fall away; and the worst," she continued, "was this very often, that people were living with a hidden power of work and of help in them which they could not apply, which they scarcely estimated. We ought to respect our influence," she said. "We know by our own experience how very much others affect our lives, and we must remember that we in turn must have the same effect upon others."

I cannot but recall at the same time what another friend once told me of George Eliot's vivid suffering and susceptibility to outer influences, to criticism. People of an imaginative nature buy their experience dearly, and perhaps over-estimate the importance of the opinions which disturb them. Miss Brontë suffered much in the same way, and I have known similar instances even among literary men. At the time when I knew George Eliot her name was famous. *Middlemarch* and *Daniel Deronda* had issued like fertilising tides, lagging sometimes, then again carrying everything along with them. She had written that noble opening chapter to *Romola*, that "Proem," as she chooses to call it, in which she stands upon the Ponte Vecchio looking over Florence and evoking its past and its present, and describing with so sure a touch "the little children in the old city making another sunlight amid the shadows of age."

I have sometimes tried to define to myself

A DISCOURSE ON MODERN SIBYLS 13

the differences between the great women-writers of my youth. George Eliot and Mrs. Oliphant seem to be Rulers in their different kingdoms of fancy; George Eliot watching her characters from afar, Mrs. Oliphant in a like way describing, but never seeming subject to, the thronging companies she evokes. Mrs. Gaskell, on the contrary, became the people she wrote about. When she wrote of Charlotte Brontë, for instance, she saw with her eyes and imbibed her impressions. In the same way in her stories she seems inspired by each character in turn, whether it is Molly Gibson or her stepmother, or Miss Matty and Miss Deborah, or shall we instance Philip Hepburn in *Sylvia's Lovers*, walking along the downs in the darkness, looking towards the lights in the distant valley and listening to the clang of the New Year bells?

Currer Bell wrote some years before George Eliot began to publish. There is an amusing and indignant letter addressed to George Lewes in 1850, when Currer Bell, in correspondence with him, complains of a review (in the *Edinburgh*) he had written of her work. Some one once asked Miss Yonge what she felt when the reviewers cut her up. She laughed, and said: "Well, I don't cry all day long as Miss Brontë does when she reads an adverse review." But Miss Brontë's standard is quite different from Miss Yonge's.[1] For her everybody struck a note, and was to be reckoned with. She concludes her letter to Lewes in these words:

"I shake hands with you, you have excellent points, you can be generous. I still feel angry and think I do well to be angry, but it is the anger one experiences for rough play rather than foul play. I am yours with a certain respect and more chagrin, CURRER BELL."

Endless histories of the Brontës have been written of late, but the stories of *Jane Eyre*, of *Shirley*, of *Villette*, are each in turn biographies of Charlotte Brontë and of her sisters, told by her with that passion which coloured everything she touched. We have no need to be taught

---

[1] There is a pretty story told in Mrs. Romanes' *Life*, of Charlotte Yonge being frightened by the popularity of *The Heir of Redclyffe*, and going to consult Keble, fearing her own undue elation. "Do you care for such things?" said kind Keble; and then he quoted the concluding words of the 90th Psalm; "Prosper Thou the work of our hands upon us, O prosper Thou our handiwork."

to admire her. She was a Sibyl indeed with oracles at her command. She flashed her inspirations upon her readers, and all through the sadness of her life and its surroundings one realises the passionate love which pervaded it, both for the people who belonged to her, and the places and things to which she belonged.[1] She was a poet. She owned, as only poets can own, the world all round about her. The freehold of the fells and the moors was hers, and of the great Yorkshire vault overhead; and above all that eager heart was hers, throbbing in the little frail body.

"If you knew," she writes to a friend, "my thoughts, the dreams that absorb me, and the fiery imagination that at times eats me up, you would pity and, I dare say, despise me; but I know the treasures of the Bible, I love them and adore them, I can see the well of Life in all its clearness, but when I stoop down to drink, the pure waters fly from my lips as if I were Tantalus."

[1] *August* 1913.—Some letters from Miss Brontë to M. Héger recently published only confirm this view more and more. It would have been more to the recipient's credit if he had answered them and honourably burnt them, instead of not answering and leaving them to be printed in the *Times*.

No more spontaneous honour was ever offered by one woman of genius to another, than when Mrs. Gaskell wrote the life of Charlotte Brontë. The opening of the book is very remarkable; the wild West Riding country is there, the weather is there, the country people are made to talk—how old Tabby lives in the stone Parsonage along with the Parson and his wonderful children! We see those girls growing up as time goes on, growing into tiny gigantic women, so timid, so strong, for whom life was so great a matter, who thought the world was made for them, who faced death with such calm and courageous dignity.

Any one who has ever studied the work of the Brontës must have realised that gift of description which was theirs. I remember once being in Brussels, having lost my way, when I came to a place off the high street which was strangely familiar to me, a place where steps led from the street to a lower level; and there stood a fine old house with closed doors and shutters, and a walled garden, and summer trees overgrowing the walls. Surely this had all been seen before by me, and I had an odd impression of a figure flitting from the doorway; then I suddenly recognised the house in *Villette*, where Lucy Snow spent that long and lonely summer time. On my return to the hotel I found that I had not been mistaken. Alas! according to an article published not long ago in *Blackwood*, the Pension Héger and its inhabitants also recognised the pictures in *Villette*. I can imagine the interest and the dissatisfaction they must have given, most especially to the mistress of the establishment. The writer of the article, an American girl who had herself been at the school, describes all that M. Héger and his family told her of their admiration and respect for their pensionnaire, and their dismay when they discovered the impression they themselves had made upon her. For years afterwards, by Madame's decree, no English pupils were received into the establishment; and what they subsequently thought of the American girl's article I do not know.

As a child I can remember Charlotte Brontë talking to my father with odd inquiring glances; as a girl I heard of her from her friends and admirers. Only the other day a characteristic

story was told me by Mr. Reginald Smith.
When his father-in-law, Mr. George Smith,
wished to have Miss Brontë's portrait done, he
applied to Mr. George Richmond, the great
painter, who agreed to make the attempt, but
who found it almost impossible to catch the
likeness, so utterly dull and unresponsive was
her expression. For a long time he tried in
vain to interest her and awaken any gleam of
life; at last by chance he happened to mention
that he had seen the Duke of Wellington the
day before. Immediately the mask came to life,
the light flashed forth, and all was well.

Some years after her death I visited the shrine
to which such hundreds of pilgrims have climbed
in turn. We came from Keighley, toiling up
the steep hill at some hour when the women
were leaving their work at the mills, and the
echo of their wooden clogs, striking upon the
stones, followed us all the way. We reached
Haworth on the hill-top with its scattered
cottages and distant wolds and the grim,
stately church uprearing in the churchyard.
We stopped at the doorway of the inn, of
which we had read and which Branwell Brontë

frequented. The days of which I am speaking are so long ago that the host was still alive who had known the Brontës, and he described how Branwell used to linger in the bar late into the night, and finally be sent hurrying home by a back door and a short cross-road that leads to the parsonage. We, too, followed the road, hoping to see the rooms in the little rectory where the great visions had been evoked for all the world to wonder at. The then dwellers at the parsonage, naturally exasperated by an unending stream of uninvited visitors, refused to admit us, and, this being so, we crossed the adjacent churchyard and came to the church, where a pew-opener showed us the old pew and the monuments, and we heard her discoursing, somewhat too familiarly I thought, of those whose dead memories still outshine the living presences. Nay, the very creatures of their imaginations still seemed more alive than many of us. Who shall limit the life of visionary friends, of dream children after the dreamers are gone?

Just as archæologists trace buried cities, so I have lately heard of an American critic who has, with a personally conducted party of compatriots and Norwegians interested in books and education, followed the traces of Mrs. Gaskell's advance and travelled from America via Norway to Knutsford in Cheshire to see the actual home of Miss Mattie at "Cranford," so as to be able to describe it to the classes at home.

What a kind gift to the world was this "Cranford," that city of refuge! Charlotte Brontë, writing to Mrs. Gaskell in 1853, says of a letter: "It was as pleasant as spring showers, as reviving as a friend's visit, in short, very like a page of *Cranford*."

Cranford is no heroic school of life, no scene of passion: it is daily bread, it is merry kindness. It proves the value of little things; it is the grain of mustard seed: it reveals the mighty secret of kindness allied to gentle fun. Parson Primrose would have been at home there, so would Sir Roger de Coverley and Colonel Newcome. There should be a proposal to give the freedom of the city to certain favoured heroes and heroines—we might each select them for ourselves.

I have quoted elsewhere the description given

to me by Mrs. Murray Smith, when I asked her what she remembered of Mrs. Gaskell. She answered: "Many have written of her, nobody has ever quite expressed her as she was, nor given the *charm* of her presence, the interest of all she said, of her vivid memory and delightful companionship."

As for Charlotte Brontë, most of the later happiness of her life came from Mrs. Gaskell's protecting element of common sense and kindly friendship. "Do we not all know that true greatness is single, oblivious of self and prone to unselfish unambitious attachments?" wrote the author of *Cranford*. Her daughter, speaking of her long after, once exclaimed this was in truth her mother—simple, forgetting her own interests in trying to help others.

I have wished in this little address to recall these four well-known Sibyls of my early youth —George Eliot, Mrs. Gaskell, Currer Bell, Mrs. Oliphant. Of all these, Mrs. Oliphant's life is the one most familiar to me, and with my remembrance of her I will conclude. Her presence is still vivid for all who knew her, that white-haired, bright-eyed lady, sitting in her sunny room at Windsor, with her dogs at her feet, with flowers round about, with the happy inroads of her boys and their friends, with girls making the place merry and busy, and that curious bodyguard of older friends, somewhat jealous and intolerant of any affections of later date than their own. It was good to see her among them all, ever serene in attention and interest, the most noteworthy mistress of the house, welcoming courteously, speaking definitely and to the point with her pretty racy Scotch accent and soft tones. Her work was never-ceasing, but it scarcely seemed to interfere with her hospitable life among her associates.

I knew her abroad as well as at home. I was once staying in a hotel at Grindelwald with the Leslie Stephens. Mrs. Oliphant and her young people were there also, and our parties joined company. We used to dine together, walk together; I used to see her at her daily task, steadily continuing, notwithstanding all the interruptions of nature and human nature—the changing lights on the mountains, the exclaiming of youthful excursionists, the many temptations to leave her task. I was always struck, when I saw her writing, by her concentration and the perfect neatness of her arrangements—the tiny inkstand of prepared ink, into which she poured a few drops of water, enough for each day's work, the orderly manuscript, her delicate, fine pen. . . . When she had finished, she would come out in the evening for a saunter along the valley with Leslie Stephen and the rest of us. She was one of those people whose presence is even more than a *pleasure*, it was a stimulus; she was kindly, sympathetic, and yet answering with that chord of intelligent antagonism which is so suggestive and makes for such good talk.

She used to tell me a great deal of her past life at that time, but with a certain reserve also, and it was not until I read the Autobiography published after her death that I realised what her great cares had been. I could then understand why she had been so scornful of mental difficulties which seemed real enough to some of us, and why she always spoke bitterly of problems of thought—she who had so many practical troubles to encounter. The impression of that special time is very vivid still—the busy clatter of the Swiss village close at hand, the great surrounding mountains, the terrace where we used to sit together under the clematis in full flower, and her eyes shining as she talked on and on. I remember her once saying, when I exclaimed at something she told me, "Temperament has a great deal to do with our lives, and mine is a hopeful temper and has carried me on through terrible trials."

Some time after our visit to Grindelwald, I wrote to her to ask for a literary contribution for a friend, an editor who was ill and in great need of help. Mrs. Oliphant immediately sent a story, a charming, long, cheerful story, which (as I discovered later) had been written by her son's sick-bed, and which she gave as a gift with her bountiful hand at a time when she hardly knew where to turn for money. What friend in trouble was ever dropped or ignored by her? When her helpless brother and his children came appealing to her, she took them all into her home. The brother died, and his fine young son also died just at the opening of the career in which Mrs. Oliphant had started him, but the delicate girls survived to repay with full measure all the love they had received.

Mrs. Oliphant wrote near a hundred novels, we are told, besides her admirable criticisms and her histories, besides her reviews, and the lives of Montalembert, of Irving, and of Laurence Oliphant, her kinsman. Her books of travel about Florence, and Venice, and the Holy Land represent her holidays; as for her mystical histories, they always seem to be more like *herself* than anything else; for though she hated mental speculation, she was a believing mystic in the semblance of a dignified Scotch lady, a little cold in manner and tart in speech. Yet, as is the way with some, she too was strangely moved at times to cast away all concealment, and to pour out in writing those heart-secrets, which seem spoken, not to the world, but to the very spirit of sympathy which is in the world, when the pen runs on almost of its own accord and the human spirit cries aloud from the depths of silence.

I do not remember to have read anywhere else a description more to the point than that written by Mrs. Oliphant, towards the close of her writing, in a book which she calls *The Ways of Life*, describing "the ebb-tide"—the sudden realisation that all advance is at an end. . . . "It is a very startling discovery," she says, "to one who has perhaps been going with a tolerably full sail, without any consciousness of weakened energies or failing power, and it usually is as sudden as it is strange, though probably other people have already found it out and traced the steps of its approach. . . . But yet the ebb has its poetry too, though the colours are more sombre, and the sentiment is different. The flood, which in its rise seemed almost individual, pervaded by something like conscious life or force, becomes an abstract, relentless fate when it pours back into the deep gulf of the sea of forgetfulness. . . ."

Mrs. Oliphant has herself criticised her own work—she might have done better, she says, if she had written much less, and reached a higher level. Fancy was hers indeed, intuitive grasp of circumstance: only the very bountifulness of her gift was her temptation. "Was it love of mammon," she asks, "which impelled me to write on, or love of my children?" Would the praise of the critics have been worth the daily happiness of all those who depended on her toil for their gaiety and superfluity, those for whom she so gladly slaved, morning, noon, and late into the night? She used to sit up at her writing after every one was gone to bed, and rise again on dark winter mornings to see her boys off to their early school. At times she was weary, but again and again she was able to resume her task with renewed interest. Too often she wrote by her sons' sick-beds, in apprehension and unspeakable terror.

No one has spoken more truly of her than a friend who lived after her for a time in the pleasant Windsor Crescent house. "It is good," says Mrs. Lionel Cust, "to gather up again some memories of that vivid and charming personality, of that brave, indomitable spirit, of that amazing agility which could rise to every emergency and every crisis, which could amuse itself with the smallest interests or penetrate far into the mists of the unseen."

"As I saw her in the last years of her life," Mrs. Cust continues, "she was old, but with the dignity of a queen, and shining eyes which seemed as though they saw far into the distance. She was looking towards 'the more genial land,' waiting for the time when she would be with those again whom she had lost here, and in that steadfast hope she died."

"The one good thing I am conscious of," she wrote to her friend A. K. H. B., "is the great, calm, all-sustaining sense of a Divine Unseen walking in the cool of the garden. . . ."

So much for the Torch-bearers of the Early Victorian days! Not very long ago people spoke of the rising generation knocking at the door; it seems now as if already the rising generation had ceased to knock. It has burst in, leaving the doors wide open to admit the draughts from outside, and the shouts and shrieks and the storms of discord, as well as the more harmonious echoes of natural life.

The impatient effects, the incoherent audacities of the post-present taste in literature, art, and music, appeal to an entirely different set of feelings from those which existed in my own time.

I cannot think they will ever impress our

children as *our* familiar visions have impressed us, and will still impress those who are yet to live. I heard of a great leader of modern ideas exclaiming the other day, "We are living in the present: why go on constantly dwelling on the past?" But he was speaking to a young woman at the time, and an old one might have answered him, "Because, as you yourself have sung in 'Lest we Forget,' the past holds us in its noble grip and it *is* the present."

This paper was written far from home, at Venice, in the spring of 1912, in a window of the Palazzo Barbaro, that benevolent house most beautiful, where so many of us have been received and entertained in kindness. From its windows, morning after morning, one might watch beneath the pale blue heaven, a sweet advancing angel brightening every instant in annunciation of the day to come, divinest lights changing into sunshine, morning clouds trailing towards a distant duomo, while doves were calling, and bells sounding for the dawn.

Just opposite, across the Grand Canal, stands another palace, also with carved balconies and ancient windows and sunlit terraces. This palace belongs to a lady who, loving good English and beauty of style, has chosen to bestow here in London a yearly prize of a hundred pieces of gold, to be won in fair combat by literary aspirants, young knights of the pen, and with this pleasant fact I am glad to conclude my little discourse about writers.

CHARLES DICKENS AS I REMEMBER HIM

READERS of my father's poems will remember those charming lines "Mrs. Katherine's Lantern," published with the other ballads. The lines are so well known I need scarcely quote them again.

To K. E.

I am just from Hanway Court,
Where the Israelites resort,
And this lamp I've brought with me.
Madam, on its pane you'll see,
The initials K. and E.

. . . . .

Full a hundred years are gone
Since the little beacon shone
On a Venice balcony;
There on summer nights it hung,
And the lovers came and sung
To their beautiful K. E.

Hush! in the canal below
Don't you hear the plash of row'rs?
Now they rest upon their oars
Underneath the lantern's glow,

And a thrilling voice begins,
To the sound of mandolins,
Begins singing of amore
And delire and dolore,
O the ravishing tenore.

Lady, do you know the tune?
Ah, we all of us have hummed it;
I've an old guitar has thrummed it
Under many a changing moon.

. . . . .

Shall I try it? Do-Re-Mi-
What is this? Ma foi, the fact is
That my hand is out of practice,
And my poor old fiddle cracked is;
And a man—I let the truth out—
Who's had almost every tooth out,
Cannot sing as once he sung,
When he was young as you are young,
When he was young and lutes were strung
And love lamp in the casement hung.

When K. E. asked me the other day what I could remember of her own father, Charles Dickens, whose centenary is being kept this year, I answered that I had lived all my life in his company, but I could almost count the occasions of actually meeting him upon my fingers. And yet, as I have said elsewhere, it is curious to remember, considering how rarely we met and what a long way off we lived from one another, the important part the Dickens household seemed to play in our early life. The little girls were just about our own ages; K. E. and my sister were the same age; Mary Dickens, whom my father also liked to praise, paired off with me. The Dickens books were no less a part of our home than our father's own books. Mr. Pickwick, Little Nell, Nicholas Nickleby and the glorious company to which they all belonged, lived with us no less than did Becky and Dobbin and Major Pendennis and the beloved inhabitants of Fairoaks.

I have a letter dated Devonshire Terrace, Sunday, the 9th of January 1848, which I am glad to have. It concerns a criticism — most probably that of the *Christmas Carol* which my father so greatly admired. It is the letter of one generous young man to another:

"My dear Thackeray," it says, "I need not tell you that I have been delighted and cut tenderly to the heart by your generous letter. You would never have written it if you had not known how truly and heartily I should feel it. I will only say that the spirit in which I read it was worthy of the spirit in which you wrote it, and that I believe there is nothing in the world, or out of it, to which I am so sensitive as the least mark of such a manly and gallant regard.

". . . I am saving up the perusal of *Vanity Fair* until I shall have done *Dombey*. Believe me, my dear fellow, I am very proud of your letter, and very happy in its receipt. If I were to pursue the subject I should come out in a style which would be full of all sorts of faults but insincerity."

The first occasion of my meeting Mr. Dickens was at the house of Charles Leslie, a painter for whom my father had a great sympathy and affection, and of whom there is a charming life by Tom Taylor. On December 31st, 1841, Leslie writes to Washington Irving in America: "Mr. Dickens tells me you urged him to become acquainted with me, for which I now send you, by him, my thanks, and every good wish of this wishing season." And it was accordingly at the Leslies' home some ten years later that my sister and I first realised Mr. Dickens himself, though only as a sort of brilliance in the room, mysteriously dominant and formless. I remember how everybody lighted up when he entered.

In this same *Life of Charles Leslie* there is also frequent mention of a certain Captain Morgan, of whom Leslie says, "It was worth going to America if only to make Captain Morgan's acquaintance." This benevolent seaman used to come and go across the Atlantic bestowing friendship, barrels of red apples and American rocking-chairs upon his sympathetic English companions, all of whom he delighted to make happy: we certainly came in for our share. My impression is that on this particular occasion a great expedition to a ship in some far distant dock had been organised, to which expedition we children were admitted at my father's request. Captain Morgan must have been on board his ship, and Mr. Dickens seemed to take command of the party which started from the Leslies' house. He was talking, arranging everything, in spirits gaily delightful —as I have said, mysteriously dominant. All comes back to my mind as I think of it, and I remember (after forgetting a great deal) that we travelled back in a railway carriage in Mr. Dickens's company late at night, dead tired, enchanted, sleepy, yet somehow carried along by his kindly brilliance.

It was soon after this that we went to some eventful children's parties in Devonshire Place, and also later to Tavistock House, and then came a year when my father was in America and we were living with our grandparents on one side of the Avenue des Champs Elysées, while the Dickens party was across the road in a little, low, old house with many windows looking out upon the flowing thoroughfare. As I look in the collection of the letters of Charles Dickens, published in 1879 by his daughter and his sister-in-law, I find more than one letter written from 49 Champs Elysées, swept away long since. One is addressed to Mr. W. H. Wills, and is dated October 21st, 1855 :—

"I have two floors here, *entresol* and first, in a doll's house, and the view without, astounding as you will say when you come. The house is on the exposition side about half a quarter of a mile above Franconi, each room has but one window, but we have no fewer than 6 rooms (besides the back ones), looking on the Champs Elysées, with the wonderful life perpetually flowing up and down . . . damage for the whole, 700 francs a month; but, sir, when Georgina, the servants, and I were here for the first night, Catherine and the rest being at Boulogne, I heard Georgie restless, turned out, asked what's the matter? 'Oh, it's dreadfully dirty, I can't sleep for the smell of my room.' Imagine all my stage-managerial energies multiplied at daybreak by a thousand; imagine the porter, the porter's wife, the porter's wife's sister, a feeble upholsterer of enormous age from round the corner, and all his workmen (4 boys) summonded. Imagine the partners in the proprietorship of the apartment, and a martial little man with Franco-Prussian beard also summonded; imagine your inimitable chief briefly explaining that dirt is not in his way, and that he is driven to madness, and that he devotes himself to no coat and a dirty face, until the apartment is thoroughly purified. Imagine co-proprietors, at first astounded, then wavering, then affected, then confiding their utmost private sorrows to the Inimitable, offering new carpets (accepted), embraces (not accepted), and really responding like French bricks. Sallow, unbrushed, unshorn, awful, stalks the Inimitable through the apartment until last night. Then all the improvements were concluded! You must picture it as the smallest place you ever saw, but as exquisitely cheerful and vivacious, clean as anything human can be, and with a moving panorama always outside which is Paris in itself."

My sister and I used to go there from time to time; celebrities and amusing people seemed always coming up and down the narrow stairs. Robert Lord Lytton I remember, Wilkie Collins, and many more with whom we had little to do, being at that time absorbed by our youth and our lessons.

In the collected letters there is a letter to Macready, dated from Folkestone on the 4th October 1855:

"My dearest Macready,—I have been hammering away in that strenuous manner at my book, that I have had leisure for scarcely any letters but such as I have been obliged to write, having a horrible temptation when I lay down my book pen to run out on the breezy downs, tear up the hills, slide down the same, and conduct myself in a frenzied manner for the relief that only exercise gives me. . . . Pray stick to that dim notion you have of coming to Paris; how delightful it would be to see your aged countenance in that capital! It will renew your youth to visit a theatre, previously dining at the Trois Frerès in company with the jocund boy who now addresses you. Do, do stick to it."

One day, I specially remember, when we had come to settle about a drawing class with our young companion K. E. (who had already found out what she liked doing), her father came into the room accompanied by a dignified person—too dignified we thought—who came forward and made some solemn remark, such as Hamlet himself might have addressed to Yorick, and then stood in an attitude in the middle of the room. The Paris springtime was at its height, there was music outside, a horse champing in the road, voices through the open window, and Mr. Macready, for it was he, tragic in attitude gravely awaiting an answer. Mr. Dickens seemed to have instantly seized the incongruity, suddenly responding with another attitude, and another oration in the Hamlet manner, so drolly and gravely, that Macready himself could not help smiling at the burlesque. My sister and I had come to settle with K. E. about a master recommended by Ary Scheffer. After Mr. Dickens and Mr. Macready had driven off again, all our plans were arranged satisfactorily, and for a time we used to meet constantly and to draw of mornings. The master Ary Scheffer had recommended, looked not unlike one of Scheffer's own designs, St. Augustine or another, with a touch of Gandish. He taught us to do gigantic ears and classic profiles; he was never tired of talking and of praising Mr. Ary Scheffer, and also in particular one of his present pupils. On one occasion we all adjourned to Ary Scheffer's actual studio to hear Mr. Dickens read; but I was wool-gathering in those days; life was too brimful of everything; I looked about at the pictures, I watched the company, I admired chivalrous Ary Scheffer's military strides; I wondered to see our drawing master, whom I had imagined so all-important, trying in vain to get into the room through a doorway (as he knew no English his presence did not greatly matter), but meanwhile, alas! I carried away little of the reading itself, so engrossed was I with the fact and the scene of it all. I am interested now, when I turn to the *Biographie Générale*, hoping to find some date for these vague reminiscences, to see how the great author was made welcome in Paris, and credited with his well-established position, and also with the mention of various ingenious books I had never heard of before. *The Cricket on the Earth* is one of them, *Chuzzlevil* is another, and to all this the critic also adds a sententious little moral: " He puts into practice the principles of philanthropy inculcated in his works."

Dickens himself has written of his pleasure in the recognition he met with at this time:

"You cannot think how pleasant it is to me to find myself generally known and liked here. If I go into a shop to buy anything, and give my card, the officiating priest or priestess brightens up, and says, 'Ah, c'est l'ecrivain célèbre; Monsieur porte un nom très distingué; je suis honoré de voir M. Dickén; je lis un des livres de Monsieur tous les jours.'" (In the *Moniteur*.)

Then he describes a man bringing some little vases, which he unpacked, and talking enthusiastically about Madame Tojare (Todgers), "Elle est précisément comme une dame que je connais à Calais."

I remember Mr. Dickens, one day long after those early times, when we were all in London again, and our friend K. E. lay dangerously ill of a fever in an old house in Sloane Street. We had gone to ask for news of her. It was an old house, panelled, and with a big well staircase, on a landing of which we met Mr. Dickens coming away from the sick-room. He was standing by a window, and he stopped us as we were going up. K. E. has told me since then that in those miserable days his very coming seemed to bring healing and peace to her as she lay, and to quiet the raging fever. He knew how critical it was, but he spoke quietly and with good courage—that curious life-giving power of his struck me then no less than always before. "When she is better," he said, "we must carry her off to her old home in the country to recover." And then he asked us with great kindness to come and to stay with him at Gad's Hill, where he was living at the time.

. . . .

There is one other meeting, a very memorable one, which I should like to note here, even though I cannot quite place it with its date and its time. About eighteen months after my father's death this same K. E. said suddenly one day to my sister and myself, "I know you will shrink from it, but I want to take you to the reading of *Copperfield* in St. James's Hall. It is the last London reading. I have your places; I asked for them to be kept for you." She was so affectionately insistent that we could not help agreeing, for she spoke with the true friend's voice, and looked with eyes that compelled us. I have always been glad to think that we went with her on that occasion. As I have said, I had only once before heard Mr. Dickens read—on that wasted occasion in the Paris studio, but on this special evening in London, it was for all the rest of my life that I heard his voice. We sat in the front, a little to the right of the platform; the great Hall was somewhat dimly lighted, considering the crowds assembled there. The slight figure (so he appeared to me) stood alone quietly facing the long rows of people. He seemed holding the great audience in some mysterious way from the empty stage. Quite immediately the story began: Copperfield and Steerforth, Yarmouth and the fishermen and Peggotty, and then the rising storm, all was there before us. . . . It was not acting, it was not music, nor harmony of sound and colour, and yet I still have an impression of all these things as I think of that occasion. The lights shone from the fisherman's home; then after laughter terror fell, the storm rose; finally, we all were breathlessly watching from the shore, and (this I remember most vividly of all) a great wave seemed to fall splashing on to the platform from overhead, carrying away everything before it, and the boat and the figure of Steerforth in his red sailor's cap fighting for his life by the mast. Some one called out; was it Mr. Dickens himself who threw up his arm? . . . It was all over, we were half-laughing, half-crying with excitement; being at that special time still very much wrought up, remembering the past, naturally our emotions took shape.

"I was determined you should hear him," said our friend Kate. "Come quick before anybody else and speak to him." And before we had recovered—it almost seemed as if we were still in the storm on the shore—she had drawn us into the room at the back of the stage, and we found ourselves standing before Mr. Dickens himself, alone again, the visions had vanished, and he was holding our hands with warmest, kindest grasp of greeting and comfort.

A DREAM OF KENSINGTON GARDENS

FOR MY GRANDCHILDREN

As the writer walked across the beautiful illuminated Kensington Gardens on a September morning not very long ago, she could not but contrast what she remembered with what she then beheld. Perhaps one of the few privileges of advancing years is the power of seeing the past and the present at the same time, and it may be perceiving each more clearly from such a contrasting standard. My present was certainly a very delightful one. A flood of light was pouring over the gardens, a thousand children were out in the sunshine—infants who could run, and those who were carried still — some clustering round the pond, others at their play under the trees. As far as I could see were the figures of happy companies. One flower-garden led to another; the gardeners were at work in the parterres belonging to the old Palace.

DREAM OF KENSINGTON GARDENS

In my youth Kensington Palace was closed to the public, but to-day a straggling stream of visitors went drifting from the Broad Walk to those open hospitable doors beyond which Queen Caroline's old panelled staircase leads into her gallery; leads from to-day into the times when the charming Queen ruled from the quaint old Court. There is her picture still hanging from the walls of the low gallery with its south windows, there is another of King George II also to be seen alongside the careful oil portrait representing the dignified and beautiful lady. A friend of mine who was lately visiting the pretty old Palace told me that, as she and her husband, Sir William R. A. (shall we call him?), were standing there and looking about them, a side door opened in one of the rooms, and from it issued another stately and charming lady of to-day—a descendant of Queen Caroline, a Princess whose home is also in Kensington Palace. She recognised my friends, and smiled and said, "I will show you what is to be seen; I have known it all my life."

We of my own generation, as children, used to play round about the old Palace. No doors were opened to us, nor did gracious Princesses appear to act as cicerones, but we knew the doorways and the gables and the quaint corners from without : the old steps and narrow passages. Specially beloved by us was the beautiful Banqueting Hall, packed full of orange trees in those long-ago days. There are four niches in the wall outside along the terrace, and our absurd delight was once to stand motionless in the niches, with some faint hope that the passers-by might suppose us to be real statues. When a timid old country lady came up to me the other day and asked me what was the fine building I was looking at, and whether she might enter, I was thinking with amusement of certain happy moments I had passed in each successive niche in turn. Which of my old friends, I wonder, most potent, grey-haired signoras, will remember them also ?

. . . . . .

Leigh Hunt recalls the picturesque figures in hoops and patches who frequented Kensington Gardens—the Court processions following the first two Georges and their attendants — the politicians in knee-breeches, and buckles, and powdered queues. He loves to go back to the days when, according to Horace Walpole, the Session in Parliament consisted chiefly of a dialogue between Pitt and Fox. He peoples Kensington once more, brings back the Duchesse de Mazarin in all her wonderful beauty at forty-five years of age, with her black Italian hair, walking along Kensington Square, and Talleyrand dwelling in that corner house which till lately rang with sweetest music evoked by dear muses of the present. He awakens the shades of Kensington Gore and its inhabitants—Wilkes issues forth from the house which once had the Grecian urn over the doorway; Wilberforce starts repeating the Hundred and Nineteenth Psalm verse by verse, as he paces the path from his home to Hyde Park Corner. But the urn is gone, and the ashes of the past scattered before the advance of time, the din of motors, and the pandemonium of progress which existed not in those days; Wilberforce himself could scarcely have finished his Psalm in peace had he only lived to-day. More than one generation, even nobler than that of which Leigh Hunt has written, divides us from them all, more than one generation has

D

enjoyed the pleasant space and fresh air, and listened in turn to the birds singing in the great sylvan playground.

Browning loved the place, and used to sit there of a morning under the trees. I can remember my father greeting him one day, as the poet advanced towards us striding along the broad path that leads from the Bayswater Road. Day after day gallant Sir Thomas Troubridge, who was wounded at Alma, used to pass, gaily active on his crutches. How often have I seen Carlyle there walking on and on, "writing his footsteps along the ways of life." One special April morning, rainy and delicious, comes to my mind at this minute. He nodded to us as we caught him up, waited for us a minute, and then, as we followed in his wake, passed on by the Palace and round by the old Banqueting House, soft showers falling through the sunshine all the way.

One hot summer-time long ago the Tennysons lived in Kensington Gore. They seemed to us to make London into a country place, so associated did the poet and his home appear to be with Freshwater and its open downs; their boys used to go galloping along the Kensington High Road on their ponies as if they were at home. Tennyson, in his cloak and hat, took long daily walks into London. It was still possible then to walk, to converse as you walked, to think of something besides the crossings.

It would be endless to try to enumerate the names which are written on the old trees of Kensington Gardens, but I should like to say something of the playfellows of my youth; of the ducks in the Round Pond; of the memory of a certain grey goose, the terror of our childhood, before whom I and my contemporaries used to fly when we went to feed the waterfowl. There was a legend that this savage, hungry goose had broken a little boy's leg, so dissatisfied was he with the piece of bread which had been thrown to him. Besides this ferocious bird, there were others in great numbers, and among them two charming little ducks, my father's special favourites. They had bright eyes and coloured faces and ornamental crests; they seemed to be of Chinese origin.

As I walked only yesterday, I had not much time to spare for the ducks of to-day, though I gave them a passing friendly glance for the sake of old times. I came home to resume my study of Leigh Hunt's two volumes, where I read of the possibilities which have been, as well as the facts which are.

Among others, Voltaire had many links with the Court of George II during his stay in England, and Queen Caroline was one of his special patrons. Leigh Hunt suggests that Watteau, as well as Voltaire, must have known Kensington Gardens—" Watteau, the glorifier of gardens *par excellence;* that is to say, of well-bred groves and glades, where the trimmer had been with his shears, and ladies and gentlemen assembled to play at shepherd and shepherdess in silk and embroidery."

The age of Watteau is long over, but as I enjoyed my morning's stroll, surely I seemed to have seen certain fanciful, dignified figures advancing, with all the graceful progression of the past; plumes waved, light scarves floated in the air, charming presences seemed to meet me from every point, from every century. . . . Was it a waking vision or a dream?

Before I quite wake up I cannot help quoting

a few passages from Walford's *Kensington*, who tells us that Lady Brownlow describes meeting Madame Récamier in Kensington Gardens. She appeared dressed *à l'antique*, a muslin gown clinging to her form like the folds of drapery on a statue. Her hair was in a plait at the back and falling in small ringlets round her face and greasy with *huile antique;* a large veil thrown over her head completed her attire, which not unnaturally caused her to be followed and stared at. Walford also quotes from the *Historical Recollections* of Thomas Smith that Mrs. Sarah Grey had a pension granted to her of £18 a year, a compensation for the death of her husband, accidentally shot by a keeper while hunting a fox in Kensington Gardens.

King William III's taste lay all in sternest clippings and rulings, and fortifications of yew. More smiling fancies followed in Queen Anne's reign.

Addison has mentioned Kensington Gardens —how often he must have passed by on his way from Holland House to Whitehall—"I think there are as many kinds of gardening as of poetry," he says; "your makers of pastures and flower-garden sare epigrammatists and sonneteers in this art; contrivers of grottos, treillages, and cascades are romantic writers: 'Wise' and 'Loudon'" (the Royal gardeners) "are our heroic poets, and if, as a critic, I may single out any passage of their works to commend I shall take notice of that part of the upper gardens at Kensington which was at first nothing but a gravel pit. It must have been a fine genius for gardening that could have thought of forming such an unsightly hollow into so beautiful an area, and to have hit the eyes with so uncommon and agreeable a scene as that which it is now wrought into."

As children, we used to play in the great alcove, so beautiful and dignified, which once stood with its back to the Kensington Road (there was also a smaller erection not far off which on the whole we preferred, for the seats were not so far from the ground). The alcove, though we did not know it then, was built by Wren of marble and brick combined, and belonged to Queen Anne's private garden, and there is a legend that the French emigrés used it as a place where mass was sung at the time.

In those days Kensington House stood behind its scrolled gates on the opposite side of the road, and the Prince de Broglie was living there with the Jesuit Fathers and the boys under their charge. The future Charles X once came to visit the Abbé Prince and the Duc de Gramont and the other exiled magnates.

Lalor Sheil describes Kensington House, to which he was sent when he first came from Ireland. It was a college established by Les Pères de la Foi—so the French Jesuits settled in England called themselves at that time. The description, quoted by Leigh Hunt, is so interesting I cannot help quoting it again:

"The Abbé de Grimaud accordingly set off for Kensington House, which is situated exactly opposite the avenue leading to the Palace. A large iron gate, wrought into rusty flowers and other fantastic forms, showed that the Jesuit school had once been the residence of some person of distinction" (a mistress of Charles II had lived there once). "It was a large, old-fashioned house, with many remains of decayed splendour; and a beautiful walk of trees ran down from the rear of the building. I saw several French boys playing, and my ears were filled with the shrill vociferations of some hundreds of little emigrants. . . . Having got this peep at the gaiety of the school, I was led with my companion to a chamber decorated with faded gilding, where I found the head of the establishment, Monsieur le Prince de Broglie. I saw in him a little, slender, and gracefully constructed Abbé; he had a gentle smile, full of suavity. . . . Monsieur le Prince had all the attitudes of the Court, and his demeanour at once put me in mind of the old régime. He welcomed my companion with tenderness, and, having heard he was about to return to France, the poor gentleman exclaimed, 'Hélas!' while the tears came into his eyes."

Lalor Sheil recalls a curious fact "that whenever news arrived of a victory won by Bonaparte, the whole school was thrown into a ferment, and I cannot forget the exultation with which the sons of the decapitated or the exile hailed the triumph of the French arms."

"Old gentlemen, the neatness of whose attire was accompanied by indications of indigence, used occasionally to visit Kensington House; their elasticity of back, the gracefulness of their well-regulated bows, and the perpetual smile upon their wrinkled and emaciated faces showed they had something to do with the *vieille Cour*, as did the embrace with which they enfolded the little marquises and counts whom they came to visit. I recollect upon one occasion having been witness to a very remarkable scene. Monsieur, as he was then, the present King of France, waited one day with a very large retinue upon the Prince de Broglie. The whole body of the schoolboys was assembled to receive him, gathered in a circle at the bottom of a flight of stone stairs. The future King of France appeared with his cortège at the top of the stairs, and the moment he was seen we all exclaimed, with a shrill shout of beardless loyalty, 'Vive le Roi.' Monsieur seemed greatly gratified by this spectacle, and in a very gracious manner went down among the boys. He asked the names of those who were about him, and when he heard them, and saw in the boys by whom he was encompassed the descendants of some of the noblest families of France, he seemed to be sensibly affected; one or two names which were associated with peculiarly melancholy recollections made him thrill. 'Hélas, mon enfant!' he used to say as some orphan was brought up to him, and he would then lean down to caress the head of a child whose parents had perished on the scaffolds of the Revolution."

MONOGRAPHS

SAINTE JEANNE FRANÇOISE DE CHANTAL

I

WE are most of us used to translating our daily impressions and fancies into pen-and-ink and pencil jottings, and to find an incontestable pleasure in so doing. But there is another entertainment still more fascinating, in which the result often outstrips the imagination—it is the process of translating the printed paragraph back again into real life. Dean Stanley says somewhere, that to see the place where a remarkable event has happened, is in a measure to live the event itself over again; and, in a like manner, to see the places of which one has been reading is a revelation—the whole book comes to life, the sentences start into sound, into colour and motion: the reality is there.

Some years ago, when the writer of this present divagation was engaged upon a translation of some of Madame de Sévigné's letters for Mrs. Oliphant's edition of Foreign Classics, she became acquainted for the first time with the story of that saintly grandmother whose virtues the Rabutins so proudly counted among their dignities, and whose name occurs in its place with the baronesses and the heiresses of blood-royal whose arms are quartered upon their ancient heraldries. The story of this strange, passionate, aspiring, practical woman is a very striking one. She left her young son, her father, her many natural ties and associations, her very sorrow and crown of widow's weeds, in order to devote her remarkable powers and enthusiastic piety to a religious life, and to the founding of convents all about France and Savoy; before her death no fewer than eighty-seven of these institutions owed their existence to her energy. A book from the London Library called *Les Filles de Sainte Chantal* still further deepened the impression made upon me by the history of this saint and of her early trials; and thus it happened that, being in Savoy once, scarce an hour's journey from Annecy, which had been her home for so long, I found myself starting on a pilgrimage to the shrine of

Ste. Chantal, travelling as pilgrims do nowadays, in the corner of a first-class railway carriage, with a return ticket. A comfortable Frenchman sat opposite to me, studying guides and maps and time-tables. In my own "Murray" I read of Annecy: "An industrious city on the north extremity of the lake; pop., 11,600; H. Verdun, H. d'Angleterre"; of a fine cheese made upon the mountains: and I borrowed "Joanne" from the Frenchman, which contains further information. St. Francis de Sales is also buried at Annecy. I tell my fellow-traveller that I am going to visit the shrines of Ste. Chantal and St. Francis, and, if possible, to catch the steamer afterwards. He does not know much about the saints; he advises me not to miss the *tour du lac*, to take a carriage by the hour, and above all, to dine at the Hôtel d'Angleterre on my return. While we converse, the train stops at a little roadside station, where stands a sportsman with huge boots, such as I have seen at the Lyceum Theatre. He has a broad hat, a gun, a splendid warlike appearance; he has shot a rabbit. Then we start off again, travelling past vineyards and villages, past rural country scenes all bounded and enclosed by swelling hills. As the train proceeds, the scene changes: a torrent is rushing down far below in a shadowy defile, between rocks heaped pile upon pile; the green and golden veils of autumn are falling from every ridge, and creepers, and straggling ivy, and unaccustomed flowers, with wild, sweet heads, are starting from the rocks, also mountain-ash trees here and there, with their red berries lighting up the shade. A sound of dashing waters is in the air, singing an accompaniment to the wheels of the railway carriages as they whirl the tourists along the heights. The tourists, with their heads at the railway carriage windows are peering down from their altitudes into the Gorge du Fier below. Presently we leave the rocks and the ravines behind us, and come to Annecy in the blazing sunshine. I followed my companion's advice, and took a little carriage at the station. The town was basking under the blue sky, with many spires and gables and weathercocks round about the stately old castle. A few minutes' drive across the place brought me to the cool, high, marble and gilded church where the two saints, St. Francis and Ste.

Chantal lie resting from the heat of the sun and from the furious winter's rages. They lie each above a golden altar, enshrined in a crystal coffin. As I come up, some schoolgirls with bandboxes, a lady carrying a carpet-bag, with two little boys in Scotch costume, advance and put down their encumbrances, and kneeling kiss a reliquary fastened to a column: it consists of a pearl-set scrap of bone, which jars somehow upon one's English notions. A lay sister in the dress of the Visitantines, who had been scrubbing a marble step, rises and quietly draws a curtain from before the crystal coffin, showing us a divine vision overhead of a dark robe spread upon a cushion, and a waxen hand among its folds. There lie all the mortal remains of Jeanne Fremyot, Baronne de Rabutin-Chantal.

It is not here in this silent marble church, however, that one can most realise that energetic spirit whose work is not over yet, but everywhere else, in the broad old streets, where the women sit beneath the arches, or lean from their windows along narrow tributaries and defiles of stone, not unlike the Gorges du Fier in their shadowy gloom Everything seemed to recall the past: the stone front of the old palace of the De Sales, with its carved balconies and facings, the Convent of the Sisters of the Visitation standing within view of the lake (and close to it, strangely enough, the window where Jean Jacques Rousseau first began to spin his web, and to glare out upon the world),—all these places seem still to echo with the voice and the steps of the woman who travelled so long, and to so much purpose. In the oldest part of the town, the house is still shown, the "Maison de la Galerie," in which she began her conventual life; and it was thither I told the coachman to drive me before visiting the convent itself. Presently the man pointed with his whip, and I got out of the carriage and looked up the old perpendicular street, at the tall houses piled each upon each, with broad eaves casting their shadows, with broken wooden galleries running along their weather-stained fronts, where rags were fluttering that seemed almost as old as the houses. Here, indeed, was a chapter come to life out of my printed book, with sounds in the air and a burning sky, with the women knitting at their doors, and the children starting

from every flight of steps. It was not quite
Italy, but almost Italy. Every one stared at
me as I went along. Once I stopped breathless
half-way up the hill, opposite a house with a
carving over the door, and "1602" cut deep
into the stone. As I looked this ancient date
seemed to become the present once again. I
myself—the remembrance of my peaceful sub-
urban home, my distant family—was nowhere,
and, as in Hans Andersen's story of *The Shoes
of Fortune*, the past was present. Who was
this coming striding down the street, with heavy
footfalls and long flapping robes? Was it St.
Francis in his well-known square cap, with
earnest looks and gestures, and dark eyes not
to be forgotten? No! it was only a dull priest
from the seminary up above, with a vacant,
indifferent face, who shrugged his worn and
greasy shoulders, pointed vaguely, and trudged
on without answering when I asked him which
was the house where Ste. Chantal had lived.
As he disappeared down the hill, an aged woman,
with a long shabby garment hanging from her
bent back, came slowly up, looking curiously at
me with a bright, inquisitive face: "Madame,

madame, you are looking for the house of *la Mère* Chantal? This is it, this is it; look at the date over the door! Oh! many come, and we show it to them all. Here is Marianne, she will tell you the same; we both live in the street—the nuns are gone." As she spoke I wondered to what order of suffering necessity these poor souls themselves belonged; to what wide community for which no dignities of renunciation and self-infliction are needed to add to the austerity of its daily rule! They hobbled into the house, and beckoned for me to follow. "Not upstairs," says Marianne; "we cannot take Madame upstairs, there are too many *locataires* for that; but Jean shall show her the place where the dead body was found." And Jean, a young locksmith in a big leather apron, appears with a spluttering candle from out of a low, arched, ground-floor room, in which he had been at work. While he was unlocking a heavy door, I gazed up the heavy stone staircase and round and about the filthy old house, and tried to imagine it in its once order and good trim, and inhabited by the saint and her faithful companions; and then I find myself descending by a black and gloomy staircase into a cellar below the level of the street. "This is where the corpse was found," says Marianne, pointing with her skinny finger to a hole in the masonry. As I looked from the black hole to the gloomy exit, I remember my purse and my gold watch, and give one wistful thought to my distant home and family as I wonder whether Jean and Marianne would have much difficulty in adding to the attractions of this interesting burying-place; but one glance at their honest faces made me ashamed of my terrors. "Have you seen enough?" says old Marianne. "Dark, isn't it? and what a hole! eh!" And so we all file up again after the candle, which Jean carefully blows out when we get to the top once more. Absurd as my hunt after associations had been, I seemed to come away from the old street with a clearer impression in my mind of the life which I was trying to realise than that which any relics, even though set in pearls, could conjure up. I could picture the determined woman, with her strong, unbending will, coming hither, leaving home and all its claims and living distractions, bent upon the sacrifice of all that remained of her past, with a selfish, irrepressible passion to serve God and to find *herself;* that motive self, in pursuit of which people are unconsciously striving all their lives long.

II

The saint, *née* Jeanne Françoise Fremyot, was married at twenty to the Baron de Rabutin-Chantal, one of the most accomplished cavaliers of the day. We read of her as much beloved, and surnamed "La Dame Parfaite." She was graceful and gay, "of a generous carriage." She left her father's house at Dijon for her husband's château at Bourbilly, whither he brought her, putting everything into her keeping —even his honour, says the recording nun; for his affairs were involved and complicated, and the task of rectifying them was a heavy one, from which the girl would have shrunk. But he appealed to her for help to enable him to be free to leave at the first call of duty, so as to serve his country and his king. Henry IV of France greatly depended upon him, and was for ever summoning him to his camp and to his court.

A day came, however, when Chantal's higher sense of duty compelled him to quit the King's service. He had been desired to carry out that which seemed to him dishonouring, and rather than obey he resigned his post. In a farewell poem addressed to the ladies of the court, this gallant seigneur dwells upon the thought of his dear wife at home, to whom he was returning.

His time with her at Bourbilly was full of peaceful happiness, but it was only too short. He had spent his life in danger, but it was a mere accident which caused his death when shooting with a friend in the woods hard by the castle. A shot miscarried. He fell mortally wounded. His wife came running to him. "Ah! madame," he said. "The decree of heaven is that we should love and that we should die."

After a while she went back to her old home in Dijon, where her father, President Fremyot, was living with her brother the Bishop. The President was a charming and gentle old man, devoted to his daughter and her children, and he welcomed them tenderly.

Unfortunately, the other grandfather, the grim Baron de Chantal, was still alive, a man of seventy-five, living at the Château de Monthelon under the domination of an evil woman, a *servante maîtresse*, as she is termed by the chronicling nun. She never left him, but with her five children wasted his means, and the great gloomy house was falling more and more into disorder and neglect. Was it fear of her, or some prick of conscience which induced the old man to write to his daughter-in-law, ordering her to come and live with him, bringing her children too, and threatening otherwise to marry immediately and disinherit them all? Jeanne thought it her duty to obey, and for seven years endured a purgatory, concealing the insults she suffered, and carefully shielding her children from the evil around them, praying with them, and teaching them, visiting the poor, inspiring and uplifting all who came near her, Even the *maîtresse servante* and her children seem in a measure to have fallen under her influence.

In this time of trouble Jeanne had a dream, in which a holy personage was revealed to her, bringing her help and inspiration. Not long afterwards St. Francis de Sales came to preach at Dijon and Madame de Chantal obtained leave from her father-in-law—not without difficulty—to go home in order to attend some of these ministrations. Her biographer, Mère de Chaugy, relates that at the very first meeting with the saintly prelate she recognised in him the vision she had seen, and she put herself under his direction.

Jeanne now found in St. Francis a friend and an adviser whom she could trust, who assisted her in all her difficulties and cares. It was not long before she took courage to pour out her heart's desires to him, and to tell him her secret aspirations after a life entirely given up to the service of God. For years past she had been meditating upon this possibility, but had not liked to speak of it, and it was to this end she had resolutely put aside all idea of re-marriage.

The Bishop's remarkable insight into other people's hearts and experiences still impresses us, as well as his unremitting and unstinting efforts to help to direct and stimulate all those depending upon him. St. Francis seems to have been a sort of Dr. Arnold among saints, with a practical genius for saving other souls as well as his own, and an especial sympathy for the young life around him. Little Marie-Aymée, Jeanne's eldest daughter, had a strong feeling for him; she used to hide behind a curtain, so as to gaze at this great Bishop, who used to call the children his *petit peuple*, his *petit ménage*, and who loved to be surrounded by them. It was by his advice that Madame de Chantal, who had been admirable but somewhat stern as a mother, now relaxed her rule, and allowed something of "that gaiety necessary for their tender spirits." "Vivez toute joyeuse," the Bishop used to say to her; "be happy in God who is your joy and your consolation." Little Marie-Aymée was a remarkable and well-grown child. Her mother had once destined her for the Life Religious; but when Marie-Aymée had reached the age of eight years, it was determined, by St. Francis' advice, and in consultation with the two grandfathers and with the child herself, that she was more fitted for the world than the cloister. St. Francis was certainly in advance of his time when he urged upon parents to respect their children's wills. Little Aymée was the delight of her aged grandfather De Chantal, and of President Fremyot. She is described as beautiful as an angel, daily kneeling in the chapel by her mother, and praying in silent orison. Very early in life her future fate was decided. On one occasion, when Madame de Chantal had followed the procession of the Holy Sacrament through the streets of Annecy, she returned, breathless with fatigue, to the Bishop's palace, and Bernard de Sales, the youngest brother of St. Francis, among other gentlemen, advanced to help her up the steps. Madame de Chantal accepted young Bernard's arm. " I shall take him for my share," she said, smiling, to one of the company; and these words, being repeated, seemed prophetic to Madame de Boisy, the mother of the De Sales brothers. When Marie-Aymée had reached the mature age of twelve years, Madame de Boisy sent St. Francis to ask the little girl's mother for her hand in marriage for Bernard, the youngest and most cherished son. Never was Madame de Chantal more troubled, more perplexed, says the history; but by degrees she came to share Madame de Boisy's ardent desires; only it required all her prayers and all her determination to persuade the two grandfathers to agree to her wishes. The President Fremyot most reluctantly consented. Writing to the Bishop, he says that only the strength of the desire of the Baroness could have withdrawn the little one from his arms, from between his knees, from before his eyes.

III

The story of the family life of the De Sales is like a fairy tale. There are five brothers living in their beautiful old castle among the mountains of Savoy, under the loving rule of their widowed mother and of St. Francis, the elder son. To him, at his father's death, fell the duty of dividing their fortune into five shares. So the old Baron had appointed. The youngest son was to take the first choice and the eldest the last. The youngest and most accomplished of the five brothers was Bernard, of whom an enthusiastic description was written at the time. "Gold was in his hair," says his biographer, "alpine snow in his complexion, azure in his eyes, dignity in his presence." He was advised to take the family home for his share, and the barony of Thorens went with it.

There is a fanciful description of the château which Richard Doyle might have depicted. Courts within courts, fountains playing, towers and terraces, the twenty-six guest chambers decorated with pictures and carvings and armorial bearings. St. Francis' description of feeding the birds there is well known. "It had been snowing, and the court was deeply covered," he wrote. "Jean came into the centre of the court and swept a little place *emmi la neige*, and he flung here and there grain to feed the pigeons, who came altogether to take their refection with admirable peace and respect. I amused myself by looking at them. You cannot believe what edification these little creatures gave me. They never said a single little word, and those who had finished their refection first flew away to wait for the others, and when these had cleared the half, a quantity of little birds who were watching came round about them, and all the pigeons who were still eating retired into a corner to leave the greater part of the room to the little birds. . . . In short, I was near tears to see the charitable simplicity of the pigeons and the confidence of the little birds on their charity. I know not if a preacher would have touched me as much."

This was the home to which Marie-Aymée was welcomed by all the De Sales and by her special protector, St. Francis.

"To see her in her home," writes Mère Chaugy, "not yet fifteen years, was a marvel, beautiful as a lovely day, with modesty in her countenance, with noble ways, yet affable and gracious to all who came to her respecting the conduct of the house."

Her subsequent history is the most pathetic imaginable. Married at fourteen, at sixteen she was mourning her first child. And before she was twenty she died, already a widow, in her mother's arms.

It was after Aymée's marriage that her mother felt the time had at last come to retire in company with certain pious ladies from the world, taking with her the two younger girls to educate. It is said that when she parted from her son, he passionately flung himself across the threshold of the door; she burst into tears as she stepped across his body; but immediately turning round, she faced her desolate family with a radiant face, and broke into a triumphant psalm.

To Marie-Aymée, who had always lived in spacious homes, the sight of the house, the Maison de la Galerie to which Ste. Chantal first retired, was a great shock. The Convent of the Visitantines, to which Ste. Chantal afterwards removed, was a pleasanter place than that dark house in the mediæval street, although saints and bishops seem to have trodden it and St. Francis himself lived there. The Convent of the Visitation stands open to the light and to the sweetness of the lake. It comes back to me still with its distant view of mountains and of summer farms, where the oxen were carting the hay and the broad chestnut trees spread their branches. The sun was beginning to sink when I came away. The towers of the castle, the gables of the old town, looked black and splendid in the foreground. Some priests were reading their breviaries on the steps of the terrace. The nuns, in the dress of Ste. Chantal, sat motionless with the light in their faces, looking after me as I departed.

They still show Ste. Chantal's room in the old Convent of the Visitation at Annecy. It is an old, sunny house, with massive walls, and with bare lights, and a tranquil, vine-wreathed garden. There was a *galerie* there too, which fell into decay long ago, and was removed; but the place cannot be much changed since the saint first came thither. There are the cross-lights in her bedroom, and the tall chimney-piece where the seven hearts are carved in stone, and over which hangs the portrait of St. Francis. "He was, for all his gentleness, a man of strong and passionate temper," said the good nun very reverently, as she showed me the old panel. At his death, they found out what restraint he had ever put upon himself: his liver was all broken into little pieces, so they declared. It was here that little Marie-Aymée must have come after her husband's departure for the army, and where St. Francis brought her the cruel news of poor Bernard's untimely death. "Hélas!" said the poor Bishop, as he hurried to the convent with his heavy tidings, "my own affliction is charged with that of our poor little one, and of our *Mère de* Chantal." When he came to Marie-Aymée, he heard her confession, and blessed her, speaking with encouraging cheerfulness. "And now, my daughter," he said, "are we not anxious to receive from the hand of God that which it is His will to inflict upon us?" "Ah, yes!" little Aymée answered, with a deep sigh; "but, alas! you have come to tell me that my husband is dead." Before many weeks, the young wife herself and her infant child had rejoined the husband. The wonder is that any one survived in those days; for we read that immediately after the birth of the baby, while the young mother lay in great suffering, all the ladies of the town came up to visit her and to condole; the nuns stood round about the poor child's bedside, and listened to her exhortations; she made her will; she was received, as she lay dying, into the Order of the Visitation, after communicating and partaking of the last unction; and then the pure spirit passed away. Poor St. Francis, saint as he was, would not meet the bereaved mother. "I know the strength of her soul," he said, "the weakness of my own," and he drove away across the fields. He spoke of *la Mère* Chantal as a saint, but of

Marie-Aymée as though she had been an angel from heaven.

As time passed, other troubles came to try the courage and the devotion of *la Mère* Chantal. Her friend St. Francis died, her son died in the flower of his age, and his daughter, the saint's little grand-daughter, afterwards Madame de Sévigné, the "Marquise of Marquises," was left an orphan. There is a strongly-marked family likeness between the portraits of the two women, when one compares them together—the same half-humorous, half-conscious smile, the same well-defined brows and full, almond-shaped eyes; but the saint's features are larger and more marked, with less of delicacy and of grace than Madame de Sévigné's. Though life's journey was long, and grew more and more weary towards the close, Ste. Chantal did not give in, or cease her interest, her exhortations, her exertions. She had lost all her children save one, that "Françoise," the "tante de Toulonjon" of whom we read in the Sévigné letters; but her adopted children were everywhere, and clamouring for her presence, her help, her advice. She feared neither famine, nor pestilence, nor fatigue;

in the depths of the last winter of her life she travelled through France. She went in a litter because of her great age. There were convents at Paris and at Moulins eagerly soliciting her presence, and the brave old saint started courageously on this long and fatiguing journey. On December 3rd, 1641, on her returning journey, she parted with her daughter, who had been travelling with her. She wished to give herself entirely to her nuns and their concerns, and also to the Duchesse de Montpensier, who had been awaiting her arrival at Moulins in order to enter *into religion*. It was on December 13th, ten days after her arrival at Moulins, that Ste. Chantal passed away in the same great serenity in which she had lived.

QUILLS FROM THE SWAN OF LICHFIELD

I

A DELIGHTFUL book published by Mr. Lucas, entitled *A Swan and Her Friends*, has been in our hands, and those among us who have laughed and felt grateful for the fun, the nonsense, the vitality, which have given so much attraction to the histories of those wonderful people living in wonderful times, may perhaps be interested to read a few more episodes from Miss Seward's grandiloquent experiences, in addition to those already quoted by Mr. Lucas himself.

It is a quarter of a century since a packet of her letters came into the present writer's possession. They had been carefully kept by the friend (Mrs. Sykes) to whom they were addressed, and from her they had descended to her daughter and her granddaughter, from whom I received them. When I first read, or attempted to read, the correspondence, it did not impress me favourably—the elegant expressions, the threefold adjectives, the emphasis and the illegibleness of all these emotions seemed too much for my patience. I put the letters away in their faded envelope and almost forgot their existence; but a quarter of a century changes one's views of life—it certainly ought to enlarge one's perceptions. When I looked at them again, time had brought to light a vein of kindly simplicity and genuine human feeling amid all the redundancies of the Muse's eloquence, and I had a daughter to help me to decipher the verbiage.

One has heard of a lion's skin used to disguise a far more useful quadruped—it is possible in the same way that the swan's feathers also mantled a domestic bird, whose cackling, as we know, is not always to be despised. Mr. Lucas asks why Anna Seward's performances, her "pontifical confidence," her floridity, and her sentimentalism, were so reverentially accepted in her time? He gives among other reasons in answer, that she was a pioneer, writing before all women had found out that they too could write. There is also the undoubted fact that Anna Seward had more initiative and spirit than most other people, either at Lichfield or in London itself; and what we human beings seek for in life, is life, and we instinctively turn to it.

No one looking at Miss Seward's portrait at the beginning of the book would at first sight feel any inclination to smile, or to venture to think of it without awe. It is that of a serious, most dignified, and majestic person, who has evidently been holding high converse. We know that Romney painted the picture during the Muse's visit to the poet Hayley. She holds a scroll in one hand; she rests her oval cheek on the other palm in a pensive attitude, more common in Miss Seward's day than now, when there are so many armchairs and cushions to lean against. Romney also painted the inkstand and the eloquent pen, and some of those vast sheets of letter-paper she loved to cover with adjectives. There are two other likenesses given; one is by Kettle, whose picture of Anna has a real individuality. She is holding an open book—poetry no doubt. Opie's picture is that of a ribbon, a head-dress, and a bouncing demoiselle, and belongs to the time when the Muse wished to be known as "Julia" among the nymphs of the hour. Her biographer quotes from a grateful poem to "Julia," by a minor poet—recent protests notwithstanding, there appear to have been minor poets in those days—

> " And basking in her cordial beams,
> The fostered Julia's form appears,
> The Goddess decked her tuneful themes,
> Soft warbling thro' revolving years."

On one occasion another admirer seems to have appropriated one of "Julia's" or Anna's elegies. There is an amusing passage written long after by Lord Byron to Thomas More, dated Ravenna, September 19, 1821:

"With respect to what Anna Seward calls 'the liberty of transcript,' when complaining of Miss Matilda Muggleton, the accomplished daughter of a choral vicar of Worcester Cathedral, who had abused the said 'liberty of transcript' by inserting in the *Malvern Mercury* Miss Seward's *Elegy on the South Pole* as her *own* production, with her *own* signature, two years after having taken a copy, by permission of the authoress—with regard, I say, to the 'liberty of transcript,' I by no means oppose an occasional copy to the benevolent few, provided it does not degenerate into such licentiousness of verb and noun as may tend to disparage my parts of speech, by the carelessness of the transcribblers."

Anna Seward was seventeen at the time when her sister was engaged to Mr. Porter, Dr. Johnson's stepson; but the poor young bride died suddenly a few days before that one fixed for her marriage. Mr. Porter, we are told, would have gladly consoled himself by a union with Anna, only she would not hear of it. In one of her letters, published in the collected correspondence, she has written a description of the young man, which fully accounts for her refusal. It was to endeavour to give comfort to the poor mother that Dr. Seward adopted Honora Sneyd, who came to live with them after Sarah's death. Honora was tenderly loved by Anna, with whom she studied, and in whose company she must have gone into Lichfield society; we hear of Honora's charms and of her admiring swains; both Thomas Day and Major André were among them, as well as the irresistible Edgeworth, who finally won her.

In 1773 Honora married Mr. Edgeworth, apparently against everybody's wishes; she would have married André several years before had her father consented. We have Miss Seward's description of Mr. Edgeworth on his wedding day, by which it will be seen that no one was very cordially pleased with the connection. A young girl in all her beauty and tenderness—a gay widower, rejoicing in his first wife's death, scarcely suggested romance, even to the most romantic.

Among the letters which were given to me, and from which I am now quoting, are several concerning Mr. Edgeworth. They are addressed to Mrs. Sykes at Westella, near Hull, and are the first of a correspondence which lasted for several years. The two friends were united by many links of affection and intimacy. The letters begin in a light and cheerful tone, growing emphatical and romantic as the friendship deepens. The first must have been written in the early spring of the year 1773.

"Your ruffles and your work-bag are finished

(says the Muse). I wish I could convey them to you, do tell me what you think would be the best way. Mr. Day is returned to England; he was in Lichfield last week, and Mr. Edgeworth is delivered from his galling yoke, 'again to life and light to rise.' Mrs. Edgeworth died of a violent fever in London; the sprightly widower is still at Lyons, unless this event has brought him over within the last fortnight."

The next epistle, dated July 27, 1773, gives us further news of Mr. Edgeworth:

"Your son will tell you, my dear Mrs. Sykes, why I have thus long delayed answering your kind and obliging letter—and that my time and thoughts were taken up by my Honora's nuptials. Saturday seven-night she became a bride in our choir, my father married her and her own gave her away, not with the best grace in the world. Mr. Sneyd and Mr. Edgeworth are too differing to like each other; the former gave Honora a thousand pounds and articles for another at his death. Mr. E. has made his first children independent of himself at the age of twenty-one, and settled upon Honora four hundred a year in case she survives him, and six hundred till her own children receive their fortunes. His estate is a clear fifteen hundred pounds a year. The joy of united hearts and hands, esteem, friendship and congenial talents, shone in the lovely faces of the charming pair. The late Mrs. Edgeworth's brother, a worthy agreeable young gentleman, came down from London on purpose, to the wedding, and spoke most warmly in the praise of Mr. Edgeworth.—We were a smart cavalcade,—and behold, Mr. Grove graciously condescended to come over to accompany his sister Honora to church. He looked a little grave, but said nothing disobliging; I was bridesmaid, the knot was tied at nine o'clock, we then adjourned to Mr. Sneyd's to breakfast. At twelve o'clock, Mr. Edgeworth took the fair sweet bride into his phaeton, and drove off triumphantly. . . . Well may he triumph, for he has obtained a matchless prize. They are now perhaps upon the sea, if prosperous winds waft gently over the happy lovers, 'And on the level deep, sleek Panope and all her sisters play.' But alas! I fear their living in Ireland—Self will still be predominant—She is happy, I bless Heaven that she is so, but she is absent and

I must mourn—that absence will perhaps be long and continual, seas may for many cheerless years e'en for life divide my Honora from her unfortunate friend whose ardent grasp every dear and precious pleasure eludes, and leaves her without one joyous hour to bless her hopes. I had a letter from Mrs. Edgeworth yesterday, dated Chester, she expresses the utmost happiness."

Marriage makes new ties and interests; it also unmakes many old ones with ruthless determination. Honora was happy, but saddest complications of feelings followed for Miss Seward, and she and Mr. Edgeworth are known to have had differences and estrangements. When at last they met, some years later, we read of the event in the following letter, which describes the Swan's extreme sensibility in eloquent terms: was there ever a more sensational meeting?

"Ah! my dear Mrs. Sykes, you would have sooth'd me with your tender pity if you had seen me receive a message from our servant last Monday evening. I was sitting in my drawing-room with a silly coxcomb of an officer who had called upon me. John opened the door and said—'Madam, Mr. and Mrs. Edgeworth are below stairs.'—Oh my Friend! I had not the least expectation of such an event—'Good God!' I exclaimed, and sunk back in my chair more dead than alive—I desired he would say I was out—a violent flood of tears reliev'd me. The macaroni was astonished, but if a thousand Fops had been present I could not have concealed my emotion. I did not intend to see them at all— it was an hour before my aunt could prevail upon me to go down, she and my mother were out when they came. I will reserve a particular description of this, to *me*—heart-rending scene for the first *tête-à-tête* I have the pleasure to share with you, since my paper will not allow me to be circumstantial *now*.

"They staid only two days in Lichfield, are now in London. The time of their return is uncertain. I have only room to assure you of the affectionate vivacity of all our desires to see you all. Our united loves attend yourself, Mr. Sykes and our young friends."

Very real anxiety for Honora's health followed, and one can imagine the pang with which Miss Seward writes on a subsequent occasion, a year or two after this agonising meeting:

"Mr. Edgeworth was in Lichfield last week, very sprightly and happy with a fine picture of Honora by Smart, drawn here two years ago, but finished lately and sent down to him only Thursday. The day it came he flew over with it to Lichfield to show it to us all. The exultation of his vanity to have possessed the original of so beautiful a portrait absorbed all shadow of regret for her danger, and it was with the utmost force that he drew a transient veil over the sunshine of his vivacity on being asked if she was not a little better. I heard of his being in Lichfield with the picture before I saw him, and burnt with impatience to behold the semblance of a face so dear. When we met, he had the cruelty to keep it some minutes in his hand. (Two or three words follow which are illegible.) The picture is beautiful, but my disappointment was extreme, for it gives me very little idea of Honora. Oh! That it had been a striking likeness! As it is, it would scarcely be any object of sufficient importance to make me ask a favour of a man who has so deeply injured me. In a fortnight he takes Honora to Bristol. If she had gone thither last spring, I firmly believe it would have saved her. Oh, that the gay heart of this man could have been persuaded to have feared *in time* for the life of her whom he . . ." (The rest of the letter is missing.)

So Honora married and died, and poor Anna put up with friendships for the rest of her life, one especially being paramount. After she became celebrated, she was made much of and her head was somewhat turned—and no wonder. Dr. Darwin admired her poetry, Mr. Saville was her special devotee, Mr. R. Sykes confided in her sympathy, Miss Marianne came to stay— and in later years Scott himself travelled many miles out of his way to call upon her in Lichfield, having, as we know, a turn for authoresses.

I have been shown some letters written by Miss Seward in 1783, not to Mrs. Sykes but to a young soldier, Mr. Hale, a friend of Major André's. Poor André was no more; Honora, too, had passed away. Miss Seward was writing her celebrated monody on Major André at the time, and she shows both feeling and discrimination when she speaks of her sorrow for André's cruel fate, and at the same time maintains the rights of those on the American side, who fought for liberty.

These letters, which have been carefully copied and noted, give a quotation from the orders of the day at New York, October 18, 1783, for providing mourning for Major André's regiment, the Queen's Rangers, to be worn in memory of an officer "whose superior integrity and uncommon ability did honour to his country and to human nature."

Miss Seward is warmly interested, as she ever was, in this new correspondent's private affairs—his marriage—his prospects. She says she would gladly accept his wife's invitation to visit them, but that she has "a vestal duty to perform, that of watching the vital flame of an aged parent who has none but her." Only Miss Seward could have thus expressed the fact of her being busy at home!

She writes as usual of her own concerns and with tender love of Honora, and also describes her devoted friendship for Mr. Savile, the friend for whom she sacrificed so much, but Dr. Johnson's hopeless illness and death cannot soften Miss Seward's aversion for him, and she even

THE SWAN OF LICHFIELD

writes of his "stern remains." No doubt Johnson also detested Miss Seward, and perhaps after all a little aversion is a very rousing element in life, and as a rule does no one very much harm.

The letters to her friend, Mrs. Sykes, touch upon every possible subject. Neighbours, politics, feelings, all are described at length; important misunderstandings as well as tender realisations are dwelt upon in turn.

One of her communications begins with a somewhat surprising announcement of her great dislike to writing letters. (One cannot help remembering the many volumes edited by Sir Walter Scott.) Anna reassures her friend's diffidence, whose pen (she modestly observes) is very far indeed from being inferior to her own, either in readiness, vivacity or elegance.

Every week she (the Muse) has seven or eight long letters to answer, and nothing could inspirit her resolutions to devote so much time to her writing, but the sweet hope of hearing soon again from those about whom she was so very much interested.

"You, my dear Mrs. Sykes (she exclaims, somewhat touchingly), are prosperous and happy, and can perpetually tell me glad tidings of yourself and all that belong to you—tidings that shall be able to steal the mourner from her woes at least for a little time. . . .

"Whenever my prospects brighten (she continues), whenever cheerfulness, peace or 'hope with eyes so fair,' revisit my bosom, like your more amiable friend, the sweet Miss Foot, I will tell you so, without considering whether or not you are a letter in my debt."

Miss Seward considers that Miss Foot "has a fine turn of thought," and she quotes as an instance a passage where Miss Foot desired Mrs. Sykes "not to look upon the present which she sends her as an emblem of her affection, but rather of those agreeable hours passed together, resembling well the flower of the fields—as sweet, as fair, as perishable!" Is it possible that the world has missed in Miss Foot a second Miss Anna Seward?

The next long and closely written page is taken up by a transcription of a passage from "Oscian" beginning: "The flower hangs its heavy head, waving at times to the gale." There is also a final allusion to Miss Foot as "a fair enthusiast, triumphant over all the pangs of struggling nature and sublunary disappointments." Anna Seward, Muse though she is, does not rise altogether above the pangs of human jealousy.

Storms were in the air, the devoted friends had serious misunderstandings; explanations, recapitulations, running over many pages, but passionate always.

"I must regret, but I will not resent your silence, my dear Mrs. Sykes, while still, though late, you assure me that it does not arise from a diminution of that friendship with which you honour me—a blessing which I could ill spare from the scanty hoard of happiness allotted to me by fate; resolved to be convinced that you love me, I give you credit for the ingenious jocularity of your speech."

Our poetess is not quite convinced, though glad to hear that health and prosperity and joy continue to diffuse their blessings on dear Westella, where, as she remarks, "The olive branches increase in beauty, excellence and strength." Of one of the children, Joe, we read, "his perception is lively, his mind ingenuous, his person lovely." "May never the blight of disease, the vapours of folly, or the canker of vice shed baneful influence over the children of such care." Three attributes at least are generally necessary to every statement. We presently come to a fading page of criticism concerning Lord Chesterfield's letters: "It would perhaps have been better for the youth of England if they had never been written, as they tend to destroy that virtuous, that romantic enthusiasm of youth where benevolence is fired by generous credulity, and morality preserved by passionate affection."

If any occasional misunderstanding arises between Miss Seward and Mrs. Sykes, it is often explained away by a burst of eloquence.

"So I find Mr. R. Sykes is entered at Trinity College (says Miss Seward to her friend). Oh, may his conduct there and through every situation of life be such as shall answer the anxious wishes of his solicitous and indulgent parents. Believe me, you were mistaken if you thought I supposed he has not indulgent parents. All that I ever wished otherwise in either your or Mr. Sykes's conduct towards him was too nice a feeling of all his errors, and a warmth of invective against them to him, which I knew arose from an ardent desire to render him faultless, but which from my own disposition I feared was more likely to incense than to reclaim. It is very likely that I might judge wrong, and very certain that I had better have suppressed my opinion than given it, but I have no power of drawing a veil between my heart and those that are dear to it. I must hope and believe that our friend Richard has excellent qualities; gratitude perhaps may make me partial, yet I confess I tremble for him—how very dangerous the first steps into life for a young man of strong passions! How numerous the snares which will be spread by the libertines to lure him to their dissolute paths! . . . I make no doubt that Richard did very much exaggerate what you said of the unreality of my regret to part from you all, but it was not unreal. I never yet knew hypocrisy, and I had been most ungrateful if I had not felt grief to leave those whom I felt had been so kind to me. Again, dear Mrs. Sykes, you have entirely mistaken my meaning. Good God! How could you suppose that the description of parental tyranny transcribed from the *Rambler* was in the least degree aimed at you and Mr. Sykes! You and I both love argument, and you have often asserted to me how all parents must necessarily study their children's happiness, that where misunderstandings existed between parents and children, the fault was almost always in the children. I thought this a hard and partial argument, and when I met with that *Rambler* which made so much for my side of the question, that parents were often arbitrary and unreasonable, as children undutiful, I could not help transcribing it to show that a man of exalted sense and deepest observation and long knowledge of the human heart was of my opinion. . . .

"The best and purest kind of charity is candour, that hopeth all things, with tender sympathy and soft consideration; when we consider the hopeless state of man, the imbecility of children, the numerous evils of riper years, the unhappy force of native and violent passions, the racks of disease, the wounds of oppression, the insults of contumely, the misrepresentations of injustice, and the bitter pangs of inevitable poverty, sorrow that brings in insanity, or leads by slow steps to the grave, when we reflect upon these evils which may some or all be the lot of every individual, however gay and elate with present prosperity, surely there is no virtue so necessary, so little to be dispensed with, as Humanity! How are Mrs. Collins's spirits? Richard tells me Miss Collins is well."

What a golden age must this have been for Lichfield when Anna casually remarks in conclusion:

"We have had another genius among us; he stayed only a week.

"Yours faithfully and affectionately."

The various collateral items of news which the writer of all these letters gives (outside the description of her own feelings) are interesting to the dilettante of to-day who has made any acquaintance with the age in which Miss Anna Seward flourished. Flourishing is the word which undoubtedly describes Miss Seward in 1776, notwithstanding the troubles which had so lately fallen upon Great Britain, and which were still gathering, though as yet the shadow had not reached Lichfield.

"It is not *our* Mr. Day," the sprightly lady says, "who is going to Bengal—no, no! Catch him if you can at receiving emoluments from Government." Then she alludes to the York mail which has been robbed, "by which Mr. Sykes has lost £100, and she has missed a letter from her dear, dear Mrs. Sykes." Then she glances at Miss Twig's amours—rejoices "in the happiness of her friends in calling together their olive branches round their cheerful table; ah, long, very long, may this pleasure flourish and increase! Her mother had made up the beautiful cloak, which she allows Anna to wear on Sunday, not being equal to church herself."

In another letter written to Mr. Sykes, the husband of Mrs. Sykes, Miss Seward dwells "in tender transports on the hope of seeing Mrs. Sykes again, and those other kind friends, who have so highly obliged her"; she is writing "with the vilest pen that ever scored," she tells him, but she still continues to wield it, "though night creeps on apace, and the drowsie hour steals upon her. She would have written before to express her gratitude, but that she had promised to work Mr. Charles Buckeridge a waistcoat by the next Assembly. . . ."

II

The Bishop's Palace, where the Sewards lived in Lichfield, is a beautiful old Georgian dwelling on the Dean's Walk, with walled gardens and stately out-dwellings; and thither, following Honora, came somewhere about the year 1776 little Marianne Sykes as a sort of pupil and petted companion. In after-days, when Marianne grew up, she married Henry Thornton, the well-known philanthropist and member of Parliament, who was one of the leaders of the Clapham Sect, and it is her own mother's packet of letters which I received from Miss Marianne Thornton, the kind donor.

Meanwhile Miss Seward writes to Mrs. Sykes, Marianne's mother, long pages of advice concerning education.

"Since you have opportunities at Hull of having her instructed well in French and dancing, I think you will scarce persuade yourselves to send her further from you. You are perfectly capable of giving her every other accomplishment except music, which though ornamental may well be spared amidst the liberal assemblage of other endowments. I have but one reason for wishing Marianne to go further from home: it is this—lest she should contract a Provincial tone of voice; that of Yorkshire is very peculiar, and few of the genteelest people who have been educated there have been free from it. There is perhaps no outward grace so essential to a young lady as a polished manner of speaking. . . . Boarding-schools are well in this respect; the children being collected from various counties, provinciality is soon confounded and destroyed in the little Babel."

A correspondence follows both before and after the arrival of little Marianne at the Bishop's Palace. We have the description of her first arrival. "At two o'clock she *came*, healthy, plump, and blooming as the morning; she is indeed a very amiable little creature—what a benevolent intention to please at an age when most human beings think only of *being* pleased. She was so kind as to show me her mamma's last letter."

There was a well-known school in those days

THE SWAN OF LICHFIELD

kept by a certain Mrs. Lataffier, to whom, among other young maidens, Maria Edgeworth was at one time entrusted. Miss Sykes, too, had been placed under her charge, and Miss Seward criticises this lady in her correspondence with the mother:

"If Mrs. Lataffier really sees nothing that is uncommonly amiable in Marianne I am sorry for her want of discernment, I am sure she has not many such children; I believe she is an able and judicious governess, as governesses go, and one must not expect from people more accustomed to act than to reflect, the nice distinctions of right and wrong, or that they should have a lively sensibility of modest worth. Miss Sykes has very quick comprehension, an excellent memory, and I have never known a sweeter temper—if there is anything I could wish in the *slightest* degree *otherwise*, it is that she had rather more *activity;* I think there is a *little* bias towards that indolence which if *indulged* must wither all accomplishments in their bud, but the excessive sweetness which adorns this precious Blossom will sufficiently *counteract* all the bad consequences of her *little* and *only* foible.

You, my dear Mrs. Sykes, who are so well *aware* of the torpid balefulness of indolence, will take care that our sweet Marianne does not waste the seed-time of her youth without ample provision for the hereafter harvest."

Much correspondence follows in the same style:

"I am sure Marianne will be a very accomplished woman, *sure* if she is attended to—if on her return from school, the ensuing five or six years are cultivated by a *regular* plan of studies and employments, which nothing but absolute necessity suffer to interrupt—this, I know, you will take care of—and therefore, I dare be *assured* that if Psyche lives and is blessed with *health* she will not disappoint your *fondest* wishes—Mr. Brown is quite satisfied with the improvement she has made in Music since her arrival here—she has a very pretty finger and will certainly play well, with *close* and *attentive* practice. As to her reading English, it does *you* great credit, very *few grown people* read so *justly*. I am not sure that it is *possible* for her ever to read *oratorically*, I think her voice has not sufficient *power* and *variety*, perhaps her ear is *not* a *nice* one, as *you* observe, and *then* her natural *diffidence* is *against* that *animated* spirit, *necessary* to *fine* reading and speaking. This was Honora's case in every respect; she had a very quick and delicate ear, but her voice wanted *power*, and she was also too *diffident*—yet she read *elegantly*, though not *pathetically*—so will our dear girl. All the instruction on this and every *other* subject in my *power* to give her, I have a pleasure in giving. I hope the dear girl does not think me a rigid monitress, though perhaps a little too *indefatigable*, *i.e.* for that tender indolence, which is often the concomitant of *gentle spirit*.

"The weather has been so piercing, the ground so slippy, and Psyche seemed to have so little inclination to walk out, that I could not find in my heart to venture her; but that she may not want *exercise*, I have procured a battledore and shuttlecock, and she plays in the gallery half-an-hour in the morning and half-an-hour after dinner. Mr. Comber's ball, to which she had a card of invitation and a partner procured for her, was very brilliant. I never saw so much company in our Assembly Room, except at the races

—Marianne was very much admired. This Mr. Comber is a fop of fashion—an officer who was quartered here last winter, took a liking to the place, and has been in the neighbourhood, chiefly with Lord Donegal, all this winter. *He* was the Being who interrupted me, when I was writing to you last week. He often comes here and wearies me finely—but, at the Ball, fops who make lamentable *companions* are often excellent Masters of Ceremony.

. . . . . .

" If *I* had daughters, I would never suffer them to learn anything from *Mercenaries*, which I could teach them *myself*, for surely the task is most delightful when the disposition of the pupil is amiable; few are so well qualified to educate female youth, as yourself, my dear Mrs. Sykes, in all things which respect the cultivation of the *understanding* and the *virtues* —if Hull can supply you with proper masters in *Music, French, Drawing*, and dancing, I would never have wished you to send your Beloved Child to a school, but for *one* reason, the danger of her contracting the Provincial tone in speaking and reading, from the servants and from her little brothers; if Molly Broadley had every possible accomplishment, her Yorkshire dialect would for ever prevent her being an *elegant* woman—of all *externals*, in *my* opinion a polished and pleasing tone of voice is the most material."

"SATURDAY NOON, LICHFD., *Jan.* 4, 1777.

"Your most kind, most welcome packet, my *ever dear* Mrs. Sykes, has imparted to Marianne and to myself that pleasure, at once so tender and so lively which affectionate hearts must *always* feel when the precious proofs of being belov'd and esteemed by the objects of that affection, pour the sweet tide of gratitude and joy upon the mind. We have this instant finished our intellectual feast—Marianne is returned to her Forte Piano—the traces of the latent joy still play upon her countenance—Saturday afternoon I was interrupted and robbed of the hour which I had dedicated to you by a *Coxcomb*, who has employed it in edifying orations upon running horses, the elegance of gentlemen's clothes with coloured spangles, and the absolute *necessity* of wearing shoe buckles that will touch the side of the shoes on each side. We are all going out in an hour for the evening—Miss Sykes and I are neither of us dressed. The frank must set out for Hull early in the morning, so I must not attempt to comment upon your last letter, but hope to answer it at full next week! That I might be able to say with *Truth* that Miss Sykes's letter which she wrote yesterday was *wholly* her *own*, I have not altered one syllable—but, since it was finished, I pointed out to her a method of expressing the *same* sense, without using many of her words in so frequent repetition—You have, ere this, I hope, received a sad hasty scribble which I dispatched for you last Sunday morning —It will inform you precisely how my sweet Pupil and I employ ourselves—Be assur'd her mind is at present pure as when she left your Guardian arms; nor *art*, nor *pride*, nor *malice* have found the smallest harbour—But time flies —I dare not trust myself with entering *now* upon so very *interesting* a subject, therefore will only plight to you my solemn promise that I have and shall continue to bear constantly in mind the *kind* of Woman which I know you wish our sweet One to be, and that she shall *hear*, *see* and *read* nothing that shall have the remotest tendency to *counteract* the safe and quiet system which you have formed for her future conduct. You wish her to be adorned with all those accomplishments that can render her engaging and lovely, *without* endangering her peace of mind.—You had rather she was gently *humane* than passionately tender—that her address was rather modest than brilliant. Ah! I believe you are perfectly right—more of this, and a thousand other things hereafter.—We are all in good health and all attach'd to you and Mr. Sykes by Friendship, Gratitude and Love. Ever your A. SEWARD.

"*P.S.*—Mr. Brown comes most days to Miss Sykes. He was teaching her while the Fop was fatiguing me this morning. Her improvement in her Music since she came here has been rapid. —Mr. Brown says if she was to be kept to practise for six more years as much as she is at present he would *answer* for her being able to play remarkably well.

"But if Lichfield agrees with her (the writer continues), if the sweet girl finds it pleasant to be with us, if you and Mr. S. perceive that she does not neglect her *studies* while she is here, my mother and I shall plead hard with you both that these shall *not* be the *last* holidays that *we* shall long for. She and I have agreed to dedicate the whole morning to her music, her reading, and a little work—the evening she will perhaps generally be engaged in company either in my mother's parties or in mine; this afternoon she went with me to Mrs. Porter's, where we met Lady Smith, Miss Vyse, and a good deal more company; her Ladyship inquired much after Mrs. Sykes from our young friend. To-morrow she is to go with my mother and myself to a large Commerce party at Lady Smith's. At present she is, I hope, fast asleep."

In an undated letter which seems to belong to this time, Miss Seward condoles on various domestic anxieties, saying she "should have thanked Mrs. Sykes amid the tenderest embraces for her last most kind letter, if it had not been for these anxieties." She then describes an ideal curate indeed.

"My father (she says) returned out of the Peak three weeks ago, after residing there during six, in perfect health and very happy, having obtained a curate who is quite a phenomenon among curates—one of the most accomplished and most amiable young men that was ever heard of, who edifies by his virtues, who charms by his oratory, and who fascinates by his manners, who is a good Latin scholar, who writes verses finely, who draws elegantly, who speaks the modern languages fluently, who has travelled, and who has refused travelling with Lord Baltimore's son upon a stipend of four hundred pounds a year, and reserves this galaxy of virtues, talents and graces to gild and enlighten the barren rocks and deep valleys of your native home and mine."

Dr. Seward, judging from this description, must have had some of his daughter's enthusiasm for his friends. One cannot help remembering Coleridge's elegy upon his death: "Mr. Seward, Mr. Seward, I trust you are an angel, but you were an ass!"

In 1780 poor Major André died. We know how his friends at Lichfield mourned him. Miss Seward published her "Monody" in 1781. It made her famous, and she wrote to her friend in melancholy satisfaction at the sympathy she had met with :—

"I enclose a poetic epistle, which I received from an ingenious clergyman at Shrewsbury, whom I never saw nor heard of till he paid me this compliment. I think *his* poem contained some fine lines. The 11th and the 12th, the 16th and those four lines which allude to the spear of Ithuriel are in the true spirit of poetry. I send you also a very enthusiastic eulogium in prose upon the 'Monody' sent to me from Courtney Melmoth. This letter does honour to the heart, whatever it may do to the judgment of its writer, evincing that it is wholly free from that hint of envy, which Pope, with perhaps too much justice, imputes to rival authors when he complains that they 'Damn with faint praise.' This gentleman and myself have more than once been rivals for the myrtle wreath at Bath Easton. He sought my correspondence some time since, though we never saw each other. I send you also a letter from Mr. Hawkings Brown, a gentleman of considerable literary eminence, and of whose praise I am not a little proud— the more so as his politics are against my poem ;

so are also Courtney Melmoth's. *The English Chronicle and Universal Evening Post* for Thursday, March 29 (she continues), honours the 'Monody' on Major André with the amplest praise. You will smile at the enthusiastic warmth of Courtney Melmoth's encomiums, yet I think their ingenuity will make you some amends for partiality which is but too evident."

Further correspondence shows that Lichfield was not the only scene of Miss Seward's triumphs; she travelled for relaxation, she visited London, Chatsworth, Westella, Bath Easton,[1] her native village of Eyam, where at least she had hoped for rest and retirement; "but this was not to be allowed. We entered my native walls at four o'clock on Tuesday. Several of our poor neighbours shed kind tears of joy to see me

[1] In Seeley's *Life of Miss Burney* there is an amusing mention of the assemblage at Bath Easton: "A chief topic of conversation at this time in Bath was Lady Miller's vase at Bath Easton." Horace Walpole mentions this vase, and the use to which it was put: "They hold Parnassus Fair every Thursday, give out Rhymes and Themes, and all the flux at Bath contend for the prizes. A Roman vase dressed with pink ribbons and myrtles receives the poetry, which is drawn out every festival. Six judges of these Olympic Games retire and select the brightest composition." Fanny Burney's own comments on the High Priestess are severe: "Her habits are bustling, her air is mock-important, and her manners very inelegant."

again; they set the bells a-ringing in compliment to me, so I was told.

"Heavens, how little, how deplorably little, retirement has it afforded me! But however I may wish for solitude, my mind, though fatigued with attention to company, is perhaps much more unfit to feed on thoughts that voluntary move."

During her visit to London, Miss Seward tells her correspondent how she was "prevented by illness from accepting a number of pressing invitations to all the most elegant and fashionable amusements." Her friends have written to her father to request a promise of permitting her to pass some weeks in London in the spring, but she says, though he has consented, "I do not much indulge myself with hopes, his health is so very precarious and my own so far from good."

Miss Seward adds that she "would enclose some of her London friends' letters if they did not express such unbounded partiality for herself."

She not only describes the scenes she enjoys: she dwells upon the characteristics of her companions; one of her friends she writes of as "light, active, well made without being disagreeably thin, with the air not only of a gentleman, but of a man of fashion though with unpowdered hair. His hair, a fine, light shining brown, is long and flows carelessly down his shoulders." Miss Seward does not altogether approve of another *habitué*, Mr. Cunningham; her taste "demands some shaded features in the mind, some Penserosa tints in the manner"; also "his voice is a little nasal owing perhaps to his having spoken so much French in his rambles over the Continent. No news from Lichfield (she continues). Charles Buckeridge is, I suppose, so engrossed with the pleasure of a young growing attachment as to find no leisure for the cares and attentions of colder friendship." He seems to have forgotten the embroidered waistcoat.

Another friend of Miss Seward is "a gentleman of great worth, some taste for the classics, tender and fervent affection but without the graces, tall and thin, yet awkward; his features have a sorrowful stiffness and he wears a wig. Now pray do not fancy he is in love with me, for if you do, you will be quite mistaken. The folks here (she continues) have married us already; but never, never will their predictions be accomplished." It is astonishing to Miss Seward "that women dare venture to marry unsusceptible of passionate partiality for their husbands, without which that state must be miserable, at best insipid, for ever excluding each dearer, sweeter hope."

In a subsequent letter she alludes to the engagement of Thomas Day, the author of *Sandford and Merton* and Miss Milnes, the charming heiress, who consented to share his life, his cranks, his oddities, his many efforts (so ungratefully received) for the good of humanity.

"When I was in town (says Miss Seward) I found there was indubitably a love affair between Miss Milnes and Mr. Day, but it was then, and it is still, my opinion that he will do by her as by all his former mistresses—talk her out of her courage; he refines too much and has contracted an opinion from (as he thinks) experience, that women are in general contemptibly unstable. I lately met with two ladies who knew her very well. They tell me never woman was so changed, that she has broken off almost all her female friendships, sees very little company, and has lost her vivacity; tell me if you know anything of all this?"

Life is certainly very full of possibilities. Thomas Day was young no longer, he had never yet mastered the art of dancing, nor of living like anybody else. He had failed to win the affections of Honora and Elizabeth Sneyd, both of whom he admired in turn. (It was, as we know, to please Elizabeth he tried so hard to learn dancing from a Parisian master.) The orphan girls, educated with a view to his choosing eventually between them, had settled for themselves in their own rank of life, and were handsomely portioned by him. The days seemed solitary and clouding over for the good and conscientious man, when he met the amiable Miss Milnes, of whose genuine womanly feeling there can be no doubt. We have all read of their happy honeymoon upon Hampstead Heights, looking across the lovely distant weald towards the sunsets which Turner loved. Thomas Day's kind heart would have been gladdened could he have foreseen the beautiful garden city that was to arise in time, following upon beautiful visions.

III

Happy sentiment such as Thomas Day's was not for Anna Seward, but much that was happy and good fell to her share. Friendship was hers, fame beyond her deserts, a competence, a warm and generous heart. There is one episode in her life which she fully—too fully perhaps—discusses with her confidante; it is difficult not to admire the courage and constancy she showed to this fanciful infatuation, facing opposition from every quarter, and only thinking of the one person she so esteemed; we must also sympathise with the dismay of her father and her friends, unable to dissuade her from a desperate, hopeless devotion to an unfortunate gentleman, who already possessed a wife—a violent woman—living away from him. He was "the principal singer in Lichfield Cathedral," as Mr. Lucas tells us, and Miss Seward was foolish "even to the extent of purchasing a house for Mr. Saville, and defying that 'aged nurseling' her father. Had Miss Seward been the kind of sinner that those who ostracised her affected to think," her biographer continues, "she would not have been so free with the praises of her 'Giovanni' in all her letters, no matter to whom they were written."

Miss Seward opens out her very inmost heart to Mrs. Sykes, who seems to have tried to remonstrate.

"My tender, unabating and hopeless affection (the Swan declares) is precisely what it was; to converse sometimes with the most amiable of created beings makes up the sum total of my happiness—a scanty, scanty store—the rest of my days are passed in uninterrupted wishes to prolong and to restore those fleeting moments, surrounded as they are with danger and inquietude; he is sincere, and faithful, and good. He has lately had an offer of great emolument in his profession from the Bishop of Kildare, if he would go to Dublin. He has rejected it. Do not chide, do not deplore this rejection, my sweet Mrs. Sykes, the total separation would have broken both our hearts. He is at least no selfish, no summer-day friend; favour and fortune cannot bribe him to forsake me.

"Has the translation of Petrarch's works reached you yet? They are charming even in the translation—how I revere, how I idolise the memory of that man—how commiserate his situation—passionately attached to his Laura for nineteen years, and mourning over her grave till the last hour of his life; spotless and amiable constancy, triumphant over every opposition of cruel fate! She was married to another at the time he first beheld her, and she wore the fatal chain till the last moment of her existence; she died of the plague on the same day of the month, as in the year on which Petrarch first beheld her nineteen years before. . . . I conceived a strong and early prejudice in favour of Petrarch from Lord Lyttelton's 'Monody,' which I could say by heart at twelve years old. Little did I then imagine that my fate would be so similar to Petrarch's."

Lord Lyttelton thus apostrophises Petrarch:

" Arise, O Petrarch, from the Elysian bowers
   With never fading beauties crowned, and fragrant with
      ambrosial flowers,
   Where to thy Laura thou again art joined; arise, and hither
      bring the silver lyre,
   Tuned by thy skilful hand to the soft notes of elegant desire,
   With which o'er many a land was spread the fame of thy
      disastrous love.
   To me resign the vocal shell," &c., &c.

The quotation ends up by calling upon rough mountain oaks and desert rocks to be moved to pity.

Poor Miss Seward seems in the like sad mood; she concludes by saying that "sweet Mrs. Coltman's spirits are also very much afflicted," and there the page breaks off.

"I do not take your solicitations ill, but it is not in my power to comply with them (she writes again). The Dean did make an offer of continuing to Saville the income of his place in this church, if he would remove from Lichfield; but the Dean is extremely old, and he can only engage for this during his life. Saville knew I could not bear a total separation, and sent an absolute refusal to listen to the proposal before it was even made.—It is true he has offered to leave Lichfield if I could make myself easy, not for his own sake, for he assures me that it would cost him his own life, and I am sure it would cost me mine. There is no evil can happen to me so heavy and insupportable as the knowledge that in all human probability I shall never behold him more. I have thought deeply upon this subject, and can never be persuaded that it is my duty to renounce the sight of him, and those little transient conversations we sometimes have, or that there would be any virtue in doing it, therefore I could never expect the reward you mention of Heaven for bringing such insupportable torture upon myself; even if I believed that Providence made all worthy people happy here, which that it does *not*, every day's experience evinces. You ask me if I am so selfish that, being precluded happiness myself, I can find no comfort in promoting that of others? I am not selfish, but when I have totally lost the very sight of him in whose dear ideal my soul only lives, I should be from that moment incapable of comfort or distraction. My dear, dear Honora would look upon my death as the very worst evil that could happen to me. She knows this must be my portion if he leaves me utterly, therefore she does not urge it. I love Saville for his virtues . . . he cannot be my husband, but no law of earth or heaven forbids that he should be my friend, and debars us from the liberty of conversing together while that conversation is innocent. The world has no right to suppose it otherwise; if it will be so unjust we cannot help it. Its severest censure we should both look upon as a less misfortune than that of seeing each other no more. Thank you for endeavouring to guard my dear Mrs. Coltman's mind from receiving ill impressions of me, but I am afraid your kind care has been in vain.

"Adieu, my dear Mrs. Sykes, adieu!"

One very melancholy page, undated, unsigned, gives us a further insight into the troubles of the poor Muse's life at that time, and of the price she at any rate had to pay for emulating Petrarch, who does not seem to have suffered in the same way.

"I know there are a set of people in Lichfield (she says) who endeavour to injure me by every means in their power; the natural malignity of mankind furnishes them with ample means of doing so; my father's conduct in caressing these people aids their mischief, and stamps some colour of credit upon their thousand falsehoods. I am not angry at the credulity of the indifferent, but in those who have professed themselves my friends, and who have every reason to believe me incapable of vileness, with whatever indiscreet fervour I may attach myself, such credulity is injurious and highly unjust. Mr. —— was by no means civil to me when I was last at Westella, but of absolute personal affront I had no reason to complain, as you say, until we met at Keddleston. . . . Resentful I am, but not malicious (continues the poor soul), though few have received more or deeper injuries than myself!"

Into this description of Miss Seward's feelings comes ·a curious item of news casually alluded to. "It is a week since this long letter was begun," she continues; "the interval has confirmed the news of Jones's[1] depredations in Hull Harbour. Breakfasting at Lady Gresley's last Saturday—I saw Sir George Bromley, who con-

---

[1] It was in 1778 that Paul Jones was making his raids upon the coast of England. The following is an extract from the *Westminster Gazette* of June 18, 1909 :—

JOHN PAUL JONES'S LOG-BOOK.

NEW YORK, *Thursday*.—The interesting announcement comes from Boston that the log-book of the *Ranger*, which was commanded by Captain John Paul Jones, has just been discovered in that city. The log-book is almost entirely in the handwriting of the famous privateer, and forms a most valuable addition to the few relics now existing of the man who wrought such enormous damage to British commerce during the War of Independence.

firmed the report—I hope Mr. Sykes and you have suffered no material injury." She then immediately returns to her own feelings.

She is delicate, she says, of intruding upon any person either her company or her letters; her books and her needles have no ears to imbibe malicious reports. "I can calmly live with them," she says, "if all the world should fly me." Some music and a hearing-trumpet were sent by Miss Seward to old Mrs. Johnson of Lichfield, and had procured a "kind letter of much more acknowledgment than the trifles merited." But she gives a melancholy list of all the people who avoid her, headed by the Sneyds, "most cruel fact of all."

"It is certain that Mr. Edgeworth has extinguished all regard for us in the breast of his wife, my tenderness for whom (she adds) was one of the earliest habits of my mind and can never, never be dissolved. When the sun is set in the horizon, and the twilight but faintly bears the traces of departed radiance, my imagination loves to trace the form of the clouds into a resemblance of the plains around Westella; sometimes a line of light dividing two dark clouds presents a lively picture of that river 'the long lustre of whose silver line," &c. &c.

Her former admirers are naturally the most severe critics concerning her feelings, and, as she observes, it is "indeed very hard to have Mr. Porter and a parcel of indifferent spectators' opinions taken upon the state of my heart, rather than my own declaration on the subject. Are not people for ever imputing attachments to all single people of different sexes who converse together? (Poor Miss Seward!) Mr. —— (she says) chose to amuse himself with the enthusiastic credulity and exalted ideas of friendship which he discovered to be the leading features of my disposition. . . . He does not plead any falsehood or ill-treatment received from me—had he any right to pass from the extreme of professions of an amity which should never know change to that of cruel scorn and unmerited insolence upon the report of others? From them he learnt that my attachment to Mr. Saville was unalterable;—that I would not renounce his correspondence or society, the right of possessing his friendship which had never been forfeited by guilt. . . , Revengeful I have severely found Mr. ——. He says he has *only* traduced me to Lady Etherington, Mrs. Moses, Mr. and Mrs. Bourne, Mr. and Miss Wilberforce and the Collinses. Mr. Robinson, known by the name of the Vicar, accused me in public company, and in proof of the fact mentioned that I received enormous packets from Mr. Saville, and had been continually writing to him while I was in your family.—You see, dear Madam, of how much mischief to my fame and peace have been these unprovoked invectives, and surely it was most ungenerous to mention as a proof of criminality the long letters I invoked and received."

It must have been as an *amende honorable* for all the "severely revengeful" gossip with which Lichfield had once echoed, that the Dean and Chapter allowed Miss Seward—when Saville died in 1803—to put up the "hundred pound" monument she tells us of to his memory—"the beautiful antique urn" she describes, with "the column of smoke which ascends from it, emblematic of exhaling life." When she herself was dying she begged to be laid beside her faithful friend in the vault on the south side of Lichfield Cathedral, but this wish was disregarded, and she rests with her parents. The guide-book of those days stated that a Mr. Walter Scott wrote the lines commemorating her filial piety.

That same Walter Scott, in a letter to Sir George Beaumont, says: "I had a letter from Wordsworth the other day on an odd eno' subject. When we went down to the country together in 1805, Miss Wordsworth thinks they went with me to wait on Miss Seward at Lichfield. Wordsworth contends they did not see her, and I, the referee, am unable to settle the point. Such is human evidence!" But we have Miss Seward writing to Carey, the translator of Dante, in May 1807: "On Friday last the positively great Walter Scott came like a sunbeam to my dwelling."

Something remains to be said of that scene where among many consolations the Swan of Lichfield sung her melodious Lament.

The Cathedral stands serene and beautiful on its rising ground. It is a century older than Westminster Abbey itself; the quaint streets lead up to the Close, and to Johnson's

THE SWAN OF LICHFIELD

market-place, which can scarcely have changed since his day. The Bishop's Palace dominates the green, among beautiful lights and shades and distant aspects. Near by broad waters reflect the banks beyond which Stowe House still stands among its cedar trees, and the gardens of rose, and avenues of hollyhock, all seeming to point to the threefold spires of the Cathedral. The owner of Stowe House was once Thomas Day, who benevolently ruled there, trying his experiments in sealing-wax on Sabrina's arms, and of tar water for the benefit of Maria Edgeworth's eyes. Hither he brought her father, Richard Edgeworth, and urged him to follow up his courtship. Hither came beautiful Honora after her marriage; Johnson and Boswell have supped in the old arched dining-hall of Stowe House; Anna Seward herself must have trod this classic ground—one can almost see them all once more.

Every day one reads of meaningless apparitions and passing visions. How much more to be realised and welcomed are the presentations of loving kindnesses not past, of fancy and fun and noble enthusiasm not over! It was to witness no witchcraft, no raising of shadows, that we all assembled at the old hall at Lichfield on September 15, 1909. The Mayor and Corporation, the reporters, the Bishop and Chapter, the townspeople, all were there, to hear of Samuel Johnson once more, and in some mysterious way moved and responding at the same moment to the generous vibration which affected the orator, Lord Rosebery, and his charmed listeners when he spoke to them of the great man who had once dwelt in the old city, and who for the moment was present again.

The Swan of Lichfield did not belong to the great; she was not of the order of Johnson and his compeers; but among all her absurdities and exaggerations a true note of human feeling exists in her letters and poems which will perhaps affect those who may not study her works, yet who cannot but recognise her warm-hearted sympathies, from which Johnson and Mr. Edgeworth alone were excepted.

MRS. JOHN TAYLOR, OF NORWICH

[*This paper was published in* Macmillan's Magazine *some years before Mrs. Ross brought out her most interesting history of* Three Generations of English Women.]

I

IN the earliest years of the present century, when Norwich was in its ascendant and giving its intellectual supper-parties; when the learned Dr. Sayers was sitting for his likeness to Opie; when Mrs. Barbauld had retired from Palgrave to the suburbs of London; when Elizabeth Gurney and her beautiful sisters, no longer galloping about the country in their riding-habits and red boots, were beginning their married lives; when little Harriet Martineau, as a child, was wandering round Castle Hill and trembling in terror at the depths below, at the sound of the sticks falling with dull thuds upon the feather-beds which the careful housewives of Norwich were beating in their doorways—in these pre-eventful times there lived in a house, not very far from Castle Hill, a friend of Mrs. Barbauld's, a quiet lady, Mrs. John Taylor by name, whose home was the resort of many of the most cultivated men of the day, and whose delightful companionship was justly prized and valued by them. People used to say it was well worth a journey to Norwich to spend an evening with Mrs. John Taylor. She was Mackintosh's friend; she was Mrs. Barbauld's dearest friend; in after days John Austin was her son-in-law; John Mill and Charles Austin were her intimates. Her life was spent in the simplest fashion. She stayed at home, she darned with wool, she read philosophy and poetry, she spoke her mind and she thought for herself, while she stitched, and marketed, and tended her children.

She was a type of a high-bred simple race of women, perhaps more common in those days than now. To some people seven children and limited means might seem a serious obstacle to high mental culture, but Mrs. Taylor and her friends were of a different way of thinking; they were not ashamed of being poor, of attending to the details of life; they were only ashamed of being shabby in spirit, of mean aspirations, of threadbare slovenly interests. The seven children, reared in a wholesome and temperate, yet liberal-minded atmosphere, went their ways in after life, well prepared for the world, fully portioned with those realities and impressions which are beyond silver and gold. The two daughters, Susan and Sarah, both married. Sarah was Mrs. Austin, the translator of Ranke, of the *Story Without an End*, which children have not yet ceased to read, the mother of Lady Duff Gordon, whose name is also well remembered. Susan, the elder daughter, became the wife of Dr. Reeve, and the mother of Mr. Henry Reeve, the editor of the *Edinburgh Review*. It was by the kindness of Mr. Henry Reeve that the writer was allowed to read many of the letters from Mrs. Taylor to her early friend, to her daughters, to Dr. Reeve, her son-in-law, the father of Henry Reeve—the faded writing flows in a still living stream of interest, solicitude, affection, anxiety, and exhortation, flowing on in even lines, and showing so much of that mingled force, of imagination and precision, which goes to make up the literary faculty.

The letters run back to the days before Mrs. Taylor's marriage, and give a vivid picture of a young lady's impressions of life a century ago; for it is more than a hundred years since Miss Susanna Cook sat down to describe what she calls a "jaunt to London," and to recapitulate all the crowding interests and delights of 1776 for the benefit of a confidante, Miss Judith Dixon, somewhat her junior in years and experience, and living tranquilly far removed from the metropolis in St. Andrew's Broad Street in Norwich.

Miss Susanna dips her pen and traces her pretty lines, and the yellow pages seem tinted still by the illumination of these bygone youthful shining mornings and evenings, and brilliant anticipations and realisations, to say nothing of the dazzling lamps of Vauxhall, which place Miss Cook does not fail to visit. The parcel of happy people (so she describes her party) consists of the young lady herself, of a "lively young divine" and his wife and three sisters; nor can Miss Susanna find too much praise for the most amiable girls she ever met; for the evenings fine beyond expression; for Vauxhall itself, which she had always admired, but which appears to her more enchanting than ever. Let us hope that the young ladies, the great-great-granddaughters of Miss Cook and her companions, still write in the same spirit and find equally balmy sights at the Earl's Court Exhibitions, the White City and elsewhere, as well as lively young divines to escort them. But this is perhaps hoping too much, for I am told the race no longer exists. Nothing, however, not even a jaunt to London, is absolutely perfect, either in this age, or in the last. "Pity me!" writes the young lady, "Garrick played Hamlet at Drury Lane last night, and we might as well have attempted to move St. Paul's as to get in. The crowd was inconceivable." Our youthful company are only consoled at the opera by the voice of the "Siren Leoni."

Susanna steadily follows up the records of her sight-seeing: she visits Wedgwood's classic potteries, which were then the fashion, she describes the models brought over by Sir William Hamilton. Her friends also take her to the Exhibition of the Royal Academy of Paintings, where the young ladies, we are told, "divert the gentlemen by delivering opinions with all the arrogance of connoisseurs."

Some of us may know Ramberg's delightful print of an exhibition at the Royal Academy some ten years later, in 1787, of which a fine copy was in the studio of our own President of 1886. As one looks at the picture, the century rolls off, the sleeping palace awakens, the ladies in their nodding plumes, the courtly gentlemen, with their well-dressed legs and swords, exchange greetings. We seem at home in the unpretending rooms with the familiar pictures on the walls (the dear little strawberry-girl is hanging there among the rest); and we can see the originals of those charming figures we all know so well depicted gazing up at their own portraits. Rules and regulations must have been less strictly measured out then than they are now, for although umbrellas did not play that important part which belongs to them at present, sticks and swords without number seem to have been boldly introduced into the gallery, to say nothing of a little dog frisking merrily in the foreground.

MRS. JOHN TAYLOR, OF NORWICH

The experience of each generation varies in turn, with its dress and peculiarities; ours is (as yet) exempt from certain trials which are feelingly alluded to by Miss Cook in her correspondence, and of which Madame d'Arblay, Mrs. Barbauld, and others also bitterly complain. The elegant ladies of Sir Joshua's powdering times certainly had their own trials. We find the young traveller warmly congratulating her friend Judith upon a marvellous escape; where other headdresses succumbed, Judith's feather had remained steady in its place. Susanna has seen many distresses occasioned by these fashionable embellishments; among the sufferers she mentions two ladies unfortunately sitting next each other at a concert, "whose heads met and becoming immediately entangled, the attempts they made to extricate themselves only increased the difficulty, until, finally, one of the fabrics was demolished." Another tragic story is that of a *belle* dancing in a *cotillon* who seems suddenly to have "lost the whole of a majestic superstructure, which rolled backwards while the company fled from the cataclysm"; one can imagine, says Miss Cook, "the falling curls and the clouds of powder, and the despair of the poor victim of this vertigo."

Susanna gives another page or two to the fashions: she describes what she calls "an anecdote upon Lady Harriet Foley which made quite a bustle." This lady appeared at Court after her marriage in a suit of white lutestring trimmed with large bunches of acorns, of which the cups had really grown upon oak-trees. The idea was immediately seized upon, the fashion adopted, and the dresses for a masquerade at Carlyle House which followed were whimsical and ridiculous to the highest degree. It must have been on this occasion that one has read of ladies appearing with whole branches of oak, roughly sawn off, and balanced on their powdered heads.

The same gift which stood Mrs. Taylor in such good stead in later life, that power of throwing herself into her surroundings, of appreciating and enjoying the gifts of others, marks her early experiences. She has a decided taste for human nature. There are so many different sorts of people, she says. Her artless enthusiasm for the lovely Miss Linley, who had been singing at Norwich, will not surprise any of those who have lately seen the enchanting portrait of the wife, mother, and grandmother of the Sheridans,—the saint, as Garrick called her a hundred years ago, and whom one might well be inclined to canonise now that the necessary hundred years are past.

II

Now and again our young traveller varies her correspondence with certain philosophical disquisitions upon the frivolous diversions in which she sees most women engaged; the idle amusements which they so ardently desire furnish her with subjects of wonder and amazement. Life was meant for better things, she says, and not least to render ourselves in all our capacities as serviceable as we possibly can. And this outward grace of good-will in the creed of the then inhabitants of Norfolk meant something very substantial, and was represented by many visible signs: kind offices, turkeys, Norfolk pippins, strings of sausages, long visits cordially welcomed from impecunious relatives, were all a part of it.

Perhaps, as these early letters flow on, the sympathetical Judith may have begun to surmise some events in prospect. There is an indefinable change in the style, there are allusions to the writer's happy lot, to a delightful succession of guests and surprises. Although Susanna declares that a certain serenity of mind is absolutely necessary to improvement, we hear of picnics, excursions, and riding parties. Her enthusiastic admiration of a moonlight night is productive of diversion to her friends, she says, who laugh at her raptures, while she rails at their want of taste. One cannot help seeing the picture, as she unconsciously sketches it in, the animated young horsewoman, the happy young company, that friend in particular who is laughing, coming along the moonlit lane. Surely it is an absorbing hour of life which has dawned for Miss Susanna; and before long, moonlight philosophy serenity of mind—all are resolved into the important fact that Mr. John Taylor, the "excellent young man to whom she is so soon to be united," has appeared upon the scene! There is finally a demure, dignified, yet warm-hearted letter from

MRS. JOHN TAYLOR, OF NORWICH

the bride, Mrs. John Taylor, to her old friend Judith, who is also married by this time, and Judith no longer, but "my dear Mrs. Beecroft." Mrs. Taylor brings the light of her own warm and happy hearth into her exhortations to her friend.

"The constant desire," she says, "of a wife of giving pleasure to her husband, makes even trifling affairs of some importance; this affords that stimulus which is so needful to keep the active mind from weariness and lassitude. I feel too much on your account, beloved friend, to salute you with the usual forms of congratulation; may as much happiness be yours as this life affords."

Mrs. Taylor herself and her husband only "wish to tread in the peaceful paths of life." Mr. Taylor was established in business at Norwich, and here he and his Susanna settled down in the year 1778 after a wedding tour to the North. They settle among their friends and their kinsfolk. In due time children begin to figure in the closely-written pages despatched to aunts and adjacent relatives, and with little John and little Richard follow the usual cate-

K

gories of a young mother's happy trials and anxious joys. Mr. Taylor's business also flourishes. They do not want for money, for their wishes are moderate enough to be fulfilled. While the children fill the little home and the cares increase, new friends gather round.

We have most of us at one time or another known the old Norse settlement, where the Danish fleets once landed, before the sea rolled back, leaving the old city of Norwich high and dry upon its hill side, with its busy interests, its pleasant homes, its lively inhabitants, whose companionship seems seasoned with a certain flavour of independent thought and a taste of Attic salt blown in from the neighbouring bays and shores and promontories; and, indeed, the life of a community within an hour's journey from the sea is one to which certain happy moods and sudden upliftings must necessarily belong. Within easy reach of Norwich stands Felbrigge, once the home of the Windhams, the "hillside-ridge," among the woods and avenues of oak, with its glorious sights of sky and sea beyond; there is also Cromer, between billows of down and broad reaches of silver sand;

MRS. JOHN TAYLOR, OF NORWICH

still nearer at hand is Earlham Hall, the birthplace of the Gurneys—that stately old house among lawns and spreading trees, where Wilberforce used to rest upon a pleasant bench which is still pointed out; whither Elizabeth Fry returned from time to time, and where we sometimes hear of Mrs. Taylor spending a summer's afternoon. At Holkham, another neighbouring place, Mr. Coke (as an epigrammatic historian tells us) was then making poor land fertile, and in return for half a million so liberally spent was destined to be set upon some ten years later by the furious Norwich mob. Mrs. Taylor speaks of visiting at Holkham, and hopes "they may enjoy themselves notwithstanding the French."

She was already popular and much made of in her own little world, and also visited by friends from other circles. Mrs. Procter remembers her own step-father, Basil Montagu, speaking with regard and admiration of the quiet Norwich lady. Another name often occurs in her letters, that of one of the most brilliant and popular men of those brilliant times, Sir James Mackintosh, for whom Madame de Staël and Napoleon (for once agreeing) both expressed their admiration. Madame de Staël used to go so far as to say that Sir James was among Englishmen the most interesting man she had ever met. On one occasion when he and Madame de Staël alone outstayed a brilliant company at Bowood, Lord Lansdowne told Mrs. Kemble that in all his life he had never heard anything to approach the varied charm of the dialogue of these two distinguished people.

Sir James Mackintosh's feeling for Mrs. Taylor must have been of a different order from that which the brilliant Corinne inspired. How homely, how genuine, are his kind words to the quiet Norwich housewife! "I ought to be made permanently better by contemplating such a mind as yours," he writes; and he dwells affectionately upon her goodness, her fidelity in friendship, that "industrious benevolence which requires a vigorous understanding and a decisive character." "The assize week brought us Mr. Mackintosh and Basil Montagu," Mrs. Taylor says in a letter to Dr. Reeve. "Mackintosh spent an evening with us alone. He was brilliant, instructive, sentimental—in fact, everything that the various powers of his mind would enable him to be."

In the little Norwich parlour, as in the Bowood drawing-room, one can imagine Mackintosh pouring out his delightful flood of talk, while Mrs. Taylor, like the princess in the fairy tale, sits listening, without time to intermit her labours. It was Lucy Aiken who used to describe how she would go on darning her sons' grey worsted stockings while she was holding her own with Brougham, or Mackintosh, or Southey—flashing out epigrams at a room full of wits.

III

The Taylors belonged to the sturdy, sensible, stoical school which flourished in the beginning of the century, amid the alarms and catastrophes all round about ; the great wars, the momentous struggles of Napoleon's ambition, the heavings of the French Revolution. This quiet English household was only in so far different from a hundred others, that its mistress was a woman possessing more strength of mind, character, and perception than falls to the lot of many.

A friend who still remembers Mrs. Taylor has

described her as follows: "I used to see Mrs. John Taylor at Mrs. Barbauld's, when I was a mere child, so that my recollections are only of her appearance and manner. She could never have been tall and handsome as her two daughters were; but she had fine dark grey eyes, and marked features. Her voice was deep-toned, her way of speaking decided and clear." Mrs. Taylor, we are told, cared little for appearances; her dress was apt to be unbecoming.

Mr. Reeve has sometimes described his grandmother in later days: actively ruling in her little kingdom, full of care and hospitality and help for others, occupied with every household interest; although delicate in health, yet toiling daily up the hill to the great Norwich market, to cater for her family, followed by a maid carrying the brimming baskets. There is something which reminds one of Mrs. Carlyle in the raciness and originality of Susanna Taylor's mind, as well as in the keen interest she gives to all the details of her home, and to the necessities of the people she comes across. She is happier than Jane Carlyle in the good and happy children growing up and around her, upon whom she can pour out all the warmth and energy of her affections.

Dr. Reeve seems to have been a sort of adopted son of the house long before his engagement to Susan the younger daughter, and to have lived and grown up among all these young people, and to have been very near the mother's heart. He is sorely missed when the time comes for his departure from among them.

"I rather envy Mr. Frenshaw," writes Mrs. Taylor, "when I see him mending pens and pouring over small print: my eyes are somewhat more bedimmed than usual, for they overflow now and then in spite of myself. Cowper says in his address to his mother's picture:

> 'Where thou art gone,
> Adieus and Farewells are a sound unknown.'

In this odd world they seem to be the most common of all words. To be sure, partings and meetings give variety to our existence; but I am now grown so dull as not to want variety. If I should wish for any, I must be contented to have it all second-hand. And so, when you have seen London and the Lakes and Edinburgh, all of which I know and have seen in former days, you may tell me what you think of them."

"Nothing at present suits my taste so well" (she says in another letter), "as Susan's Latin lessons and her philosophical old master. . . . When we get to Cicero's discussions on the nature of the soul, or Virgil's fine descriptions, my mind is filled up. Life is either a dull round of eating, drinking, and sleeping, or a spark of ethereal fire just kindled.

"Do not suppose I am beginning or ever will begin to preach to you. We know each other's opinions upon these topics, and we equally despise any shackles for the human mind but those which God and Nature impose upon us. But if we endeavour to escape from these, we certainly subject ourselves to others infinitely more galling."

What a good friend she must have been for a young man at his start in life—what a good companion! Her letters are full of charming sense, of useful and pleasant suggestions, and as one quotes at random one feels that they contain a hundred things which ought still to be said to the young, still to be felt by the old.

On one occasion, after enumerating several remarkable people, she names a certain Mr. Wishaw.

"I would not have said so much about a person you know nothing of, but for the comfortable feeling *that people of the right sort are always to be found,* and also that they are sometimes happily thrown in our way; nothing tends more to enjoyment than to keep up a taste for their company whenever and wherever it can be had, instead of fancying that excellence is the exclusive production of past times or distant parts."

Is there not a whole philosophy of good sense in all this? Mrs. Taylor was no optimist like her friend Mrs. Opie; she had no exaggerated ideas of life and its possibilities; but she fully realised what was possible, and she held faithfully and gratefully to the blessings within her grasp. She continues very warmly attached to her young correspondent. "The very feelings which have produced such a friendship must perpetuate it," she says; and few people knew better than she did what it was to possess warm and enthusiastic friends.

So she writes on, discoursing, philosophising, throwing out the suggestions of her bright and practical mind as they occur to her, and we cannot do better than to go on quoting the passages as they occur. Here is one of her sensible sententious observations.

"There is no surer way of becoming acquainted with our own mind than by the effect produced upon it by the conduct of others; if we can tolerate vice and folly, we may grow fond of them in time. Perhaps," she continues, "you can bear witness to the truth of another remark, that people generally wrap themselves up in a solemn kind of reserve, and particularly those who have taken upon themselves the task of enlightening the world. It is to be accounted for from the jealousy and fear of losing a reputation once acquired, by the unguarded frankness of colloquial intercourse. Be it ours, my dear friend, merrily to philosophise, sweetly to play the fool. Strange counsel to a young man in a grave university."

Through all the tumult of the early years of the century the Taylors' home pursues its steady life. The elder boys grow up and go out into the world; little Sally, the pet of the family, who is to translate Ranke in after life, is beginning to write in round-hand; Susan is still Mr. Frenshaw's pupil; of herself Mrs. Taylor writes:

"For my part I never valued life more than I do at present, yet I think it would be a relief to me to feel as if I could be spared; but perhaps in this I deceive myself, and one of the charms of the world may be that I am still wanted in it. It is a pleasant world after all, and for your comfort, my dear friend, let me tell you that it is not only pleasant at that delicious season which we may denominate the morning of our existence,—there is a chastened, a temperate kind of happiness, which is perhaps to the full as desirable as the more glowing sensations of our early days."

She is greatly interested in the *Edinburgh Review*, then in its earliest numbers. It was first published in 1802; Jeffrey, Brougham, and Sydney Smith were its founders, clothing the new-born potentate in the Whig colours, blue and yellow. Dr. Reeve, who had then only just taken his degree at Edinburgh, contributed some articles to the first numbers. Reviews have their own life and growth. This one toned down with time; but in its early days it was somewhat over-vigorous and unsparing in its measure. Mrs. Taylor has been reading an article on the *Life of Cowper*, and the busy lady, dispensing her loaves and fishes, still finds time to review the reviewer, and to add her own excellent comment to the text. She says:

"Mr. Hayley's style wants that majestic simplicity with which such a character as Cowper's should have been portrayed. He thinks it necessary too, as Mr. Jeffrey observes, to praise everybody. This is so like the misses who call all their insipid acquaintance 'sweet,' and 'interesting,' that it makes me rather sick. A biographer is good for nothing who does not give those touches, those lights and shadows which identify his characters;—on this account I do not like a remark of the reviewer that Mrs. Unwin's little jealousies of Lady Austen might as well have been passed over in silence. If the weaknesses of excellent people are to be concealed, how shall we form an accurate impression of human nature?"

It would certainly be difficult to tell one person from another. Again she says:

"Nothing can operate more powerfully against the attainment of excellences in every species of composition, than the indiscriminate praise, and false tenderness, which prevent those writers who are capable of higher degrees of improvement from endeavouring sedulously to aim at greater perfection, or which lead those who are incapable to trouble the public at all. I have been witness to such extravagant praises bestowed upon inferior compositions, especially in London, that I rejoice in the more hardy criticism of our northern metropolis, not from a desire to depreciate, but from a conviction that, the more completely both books and characters find their proper stations, the better it will be for society. I think the 'E. R.' contains just but not ill-natured criticism.

"If I were inclined to make an appeal for any person who has fallen under the lash, it would be for Robert Southey, whose experiments in poetry I acknowledge to be many of them fantastic and extravagant, but they are the experiments of a man of genius. . . . I think we ought to be thankful to literary pioneers. . . . After all that can be said as an apology for the new school of poets, they (themselves) must find the exact boundary between simplicity and childish puerility."

IV

One important element of daily life in England all this time must not be overlooked, and that was, the prevailing fear of a French invasion which constantly haunted people's minds. Sir George Napier, in his Memoirs, tells us that he heard from Soult himself that the project was in the Emperor's thoughts.

In Herbert Fisher's *History of Napoleon* we read of the Emperor "spending five weeks on the north coast of France in the summer of 1804, throwing the whole weight of his fiery energy into the naval preparations, and taking a strange exhilaration and excitement from the movement of the sea; of twenty millions of francs appropriated to the improvement of the roads in Picardy; and of a medal ordered to be struck representing Hercules strangling a mermaid, and bearing the legend, 'Descente en Angleterre, frappé a Londres, 1804.'"

The mermaid was not unprepared.

Mrs. Taylor describes the start of the Norwich volunteers:

"I begin to think people may make a joke of anything if they try; but I was never less disposed to be merry than this morning, when, in the midst of pouring rain, our volunteers with three cheers bade farewell to their native city; Mr. Houghton, the clergyman, gave a breakfast on the occasion by candle-light. Dear little Mary looked on with wondering eyes at her old friends transformed into soldiers. If the French land in Norfolk, I shall expect prodigies of valour from you. What do you think of Richard in his scarlet uniform? Of all things this is the last sight I should have dreamed of seeing."

The French never landed in Norfolk, but an event which Mrs. Taylor contemplates with far less equanimity is beginning to foreshadow its coming. Mr. Frenshaw's pupil is still following her Greek lessons and sewing her seams, but she is also growing up day by day and hour by hour as maidens of fifteen are apt to do, and her mother (as is the way of mothers) is among the last to realise this fact. Little Susan who leaves her dressing things behind her, who has to be reminded to tie up parcels securely, who but yesterday was a baby,—is it possible that already a woman's life and cares are awaiting her, and that the young doctor is thinking of her as a helpmate and companion for life! The extraordinary fact seems to have taken Mrs. Taylor quite by surprise. Mothers and daughters of our own time are in a different attitude from the affectionate but Minerva-like terms on which they were content to remain in the days of which we are writing. I have heard it lately said with truth, that the difference of feeling now existing between parents and children, far exceeds the natural divergence of a single generation. A whole revolution of opinion and impulse has come about within the last twenty years, dividing even young mothers from their growing daughters. It must require some generosity and intellect in a parent to discriminate between what is harmless in itself, though it may absolutely jar against her own instincts and prejudices, and that which borders upon the common and the reckless, to use no harsher words. Mothers and daughters in those days were upon terms which we can scarcely realise now. There was a decorum, a deliberation, a stiffness in their intercourse which could perhaps better be carried out before posts, telegrams, and daily papers had multiplied occupation, familiarity, and consequent haste. It was Mrs. Taylor's belief, for instance, that during her girls' absence from home "their moral improvement would keep pace with their intellectual, thanks to the observations and discussions they would receive by letter." All these grand words mean nothing more, after all, than that the mother is ever thinking, hoping, planning for her children's well-doing and safety.

Susan is, however, to know nothing of Dr. Reeve's ardent feelings; not one word is to reveal to her the romance of which the web is silently weaving about her. She is only sixteen; she is to go on with her lessons, to see something of the world, to "practise housekeeping and the culinary arts, that she may not from mere inexperience make mistakes which her husband would not like"; but no glimpse of his real feeling is to be allowed to her. One feels sorry for the poor lover, and yet how wise is the mother's appeal to him not yet to disturb her young daughter's serene and innocent mind!

"Prove," she says, "that you can, as you said to me, command your feelings. The way to allow mind and body to come to perfection is to suffer them to ripen by degrees.

"If you knew what harm it would do to substitute constrained manners for innocent frankness, and to carry forward Susan's attention to distant objects, instead of bestowing the whole force of her mind upon present subjects."

And then comes a little relenting sympathy.

"When either you or I am inclined to torment ourselves with fruitless wishes, let us have the comfort of thinking there is always one person we can sit down and open our hearts to."

The anxious mother writes page after page to her would-be son-in-law, half-scolding, half-soothing. Why does he want to settle in London? Why is he not satisfied with Norwich and Norwich life?

"Dr. Alderson," she says, "after reading me those letters of Mrs. Opie's which completely prove that the whole fraternity of authors, artists, lecturers, and publick people get such an insatiable appetite for praise, that nothing but the greatest adulation can prevent their being miserable, came to this sentence: 'Dr. Reeve, like a sensible man, prefers London to Norwich.' 'Is that a proof of sense,' said I, 'to reject what you allow is an extraordinary chance of settling to advantage in a place, because it contains but 40,000 inhabitants!'"

Meanwhile, in 1805, Mrs. Taylor gives an account of another talk with Dr. Alderson: "'What a pity it is that Dr. Reeve should not settle here,' says Dr. Alderson, 'when there is so fine an opening and nobody to fill up the vacancy at the hospital; but *London*, I suppose.' . . . 'Yes,' said I, 'he has contracted something of the disease which people acquire by living there—a sort of feeling that no other place is fit to live in.'" To which the kind old doctor replies by reminding Mrs. Taylor that he, himself, will be dead before very long, and that this is an additional reason for Dr. Reeve's return to Norwich. And very soon, and with very good reason, Dr. Reeve seems to have made up his mind, and to have given up all thought of settling away from Norwich, and, premature though it may have appeared to the poor anxious mother, he seems to have disclosed his feelings to his future wife.

Then Susan goes to London to visit Mrs. Barbauld, and improve her mind, and the engagement is formally announced. Her mother is glad she reads poetry with Mrs. Barbauld, and delighted she has been to the play. Here comes a gentle motherly rebuke:

"It would have been better if Reeve had not accompanied you to Stoke Newington; we must not only mind our P's and Q's, but our 'R's.' You know how freely I like to talk to you about everything. Do not show a kind of weakness, which in the end never fails to lower a woman, even in the estimation of a lover! Men may be gratified first by possessing unbounded influence over the mind of a woman, but they generally despise her for it in the end. One of the great evils in contracting engagements of this sort at such an early age as yours is the full disclosure of affections owing to the innocent simplicity of youth, which a woman at a more advanced period, from a due sense of propriety, would certainly in some measure have concealed. For the future show Reeve that you, like him, can bear absence when absence is necessary, and that the only way to be fit for the duties of life hereafter is to perform them with the utmost zeal and alacrity now."

How admirable is all this, how Spartan, how sensible—and how difficult to carry out! And then comes a touching little bit of sentiment on Mrs. Taylor's own account:

"Your father has just reminded me that to-morrow is my birthday. What a difference between the beginning of life and the close; solicitude on one's own account seems quite extinguished as far as relates to this world, not so for one's children. Towards them it will remain to the last moment; but I will endeavour to make it useful without being troublesome to you."

Other admonitions follow, warnings against want of attention to respectful demeanour such as is never to be observed in well-bred girls; and then, very motherlike, at the end of the letter:

"Now I have written this letter, I have a

great mind to burn it, I am so unwilling to give you a moment's pain, but if you take it as a proof of love, and determine to profit by it, it will rather give you pleasure.

"When you are absent it is a great effort to think of faults. I could rather sit down and cry for your company."

One letter winds up with a quotation from one of the lover's epistles. He complains that he has heard nothing for several weeks. And here it is not possible to sympathise as much as usual when the mother points out to the daughter that she should not encourage her lover to expect to hear more often than is convenient.

Mrs. Taylor, as other mothers have been and will be again, is still perturbed by her son-in-law's impatience, by his ineradicable conviction that two people can live at the same expense as one. Little by little, however, difficulties are removed. Mr. Reeve's father promises him a good allowance; all is made smooth for the young couple's future, and at last they are married in the autumn of 1807. A house belonging to the Kerrison family had been taken in Surrey Street. We hear of many details: linen and boilers, and pails, and brushes, and scouring-cloths; a faithful Mary is engaged, who falls ill from over-scrubbing and has to be nursed. The good mother is there ready to see to everything, to nurse, to shop, to order, She writes full and detailed accounts of everything that is in preparation for the home. "Don't you wonder we can be interested in anything," she says, "while these rivers of blood are flowing on the Continent, only to complete the triumph of a tyrant, and to rivet the chains of poor, subjugated, unhappy Europe? But nevertheless, whatever is going on round about, people happily go on being interested in their own lives, and in those belonging to them."

Perhaps the most charming letter in the whole collection is one from Mrs. Taylor to her husband, towards the end of their peaceful married life, in which, in that still steady and exquisitely finished handwriting, she treats of "the only subject of deep interest to either of them," and recapitulates the family history. There is something almost biblical in the calm outlook, in the benediction at the end of this long and loving life. "As the father and mother of seven children, we have reason to be thankful that they are what they are, and to hope that their descendants may do them as much credit, and give them as much comfort . . . that John and his wife are living in a handsome, commodious house in a polite and pleasant neighbourhood is a gratifying circumstance as far as health is concerned." Mrs. Taylor is only afraid that *their* children may not sufficiently remember that this style of living is entirely dependent upon the father's life and exertions. She next comes to her beloved Richard, "with all his valuable acquirements, his genuine humility, disinterested kindness, undeviating integrity." How wise is the manner of her wish to help him! "I know no other way to make ourselves tolerably easy about this dear clever child of ours, than to let him be the arbiter of his own destiny." She feels, she writes, "that each one of them should attain to that measure of independence which it is in the parents' power to bestow, at whatever cost to themselves." Then of another of her sons, "It would embitter my latter days if I thought that there was anything standing against Edward which would distress him, or that he should owe to the favour of his brethren what he is really entitled to from you; ... it is sometimes as much a parent's duty to deviate from the equal distribution of property as it is in general to adhere to it. What I have to give goes to Sally and Deborah, because they want it more than my other daughters." The whole letter breathes a spirit of wisdom and good sense and tender justice, and is, indeed, a model of impartiality and unselfish good judgment. The mother is ill and alone at Norwich; but she forbids the father to mention this to the son with whom he is staying. "You know how well I can bear being alone if I have but books, which I am sure never to want." It is in this same letter that Mrs. Taylor speaks of occasional talks with her "eccentric lodger" John Stuart Mill.

As time goes on Susanna Taylor softens and responds more and more to youth. For her child's child her warm heart seems to thaw the formalities of her time and age. It is touching to hear of the faithful remembrances of long-ago games at coach-and-horses, in which grand-mamma is the horse, and "darling," as she calls her little grandson, is the coachman. "But I shall have no room for love to Darling Boy," she writes somewhere; "he must have almost lost the idea of Norwich-grandmamma." The grandchild occupies her mind, and delights her heart; how proud she is of his cleverness and bright intellect; she tries to excuse her weakness on utilitarian principles, and frames a scheme in which the grandparents are to spoil in exact proportion to the parents' inflexibility.

Sally, the younger daughter, is also the mother of a little daughter, much beloved by "mamma," as she calls Mrs. Taylor. The present writer has still before her as she writes the image of Lucie, Lady Duff Gordon, that noble Spanish-looking lady of whom as Sally's baby there are such pretty details. "I understand all her language;—the rubbish drawer is her delight," says Mrs. Taylor, and then she adds, "It is time she left me, for I am growing to be too fond of Sally's child." Sally's child's child now speaks to us, a fourth generation not to be overlooked.

My story is slender enough. The figures come and go. That of the young doctor disappears far too early from the peaceful scene—peaceful it was amid the storms and catastrophes of the time, when the selfish ambitions of the ambitious could only be atoned for by the steady moderation and unselfish wisdom of the honourable unknown.

L'ART D'ÊTRE GRANDPÈRE [1]

I

THE great Hugo, Victor in Poesy, Victor in Romance, was able to win new laurels when he in his old age wrote of "L'Art d'être Grandpère." It is a knowledge which comes naturally to some, a chord struck between the happy past and the golden dawn of the days to come.

I have known others who have also lived in this beautiful region—an epiphany which some of the wisest have joined, when they come from afar with their dear and priceless gifts to bless the future, as yet unrevealed.

Just about a hundred years ago a kind old grandfather, away from the storms and terrors that rent Europe in those troubled days, sat quietly in Nassau Street,[2] off Portland Place, writing to his little grandson. The writer was

[1] Copyright, 1913, by Lady Ritchie, in the United States of America.
[2] Now Suffolk Street.

L'ART D'ÊTRE GRANDPÈRE 173

Major James Rennell of the Hon. E.I.C.S., one of the gentlest and most unaffected of men, the first great English geographer, as Sir Clements Markham has called him, a man who had measured space and oceans and traced unknown currents, who had mapped out India and Africa, whose work is still a standard of reference, and whose name was then known and held, as now, in highest esteem by all the savants of Europe. These letters of his were addressed in delicate handwriting to "Master James Rennell Rodd." They begin in 1812, and it is by the permission of my old friend and connection, Mrs. James Rennell Rodd, that I have been able to read the correspondence. The early notes are written in red ink, with plainly printed characters, to make them easy for the little boy. In sending them to me Mrs. Rodd wrote as follows:

"My husband treasured every letter his grandfather sent him; the first began on his first birthday, and until the boy could read, the little notes came following each other. Major Rennell lived a most simple, abstemious life in what was once called Nassau Street, with his old servant Mary Medley. My husband as a boy used to go and share his grandfather's afternoon coffee and toast."

Major Rennell's first letter to his grandson ran as follows (it is dated March 12, 1812):

"MY DEAR LITTLE DOUBLE NAMESAKE,—Perhaps I may be the first person who has ever approached you with a written address. I shall use no flattery, for it is the truth to say that you are one of the most blameless characters amongst us. . . . I hear much of your filial affection and that you give great comfort to your worthy parents. . . . I beg my kindest regards to your good father and mother.—Your most affectionate, G.-P."

After this introduction the letters run on, full of interest in the little fellow's childhood, in his toys and games, in his life at school, his outings and amusements; the grandfather telling him also of his own doings, his walks, the quiet daily round. All his life long Major Rennell had lived in a world of observation as well as of action, and he still notes facts and experiences likely to interest the boy and to be understood by him. He writes of the weather, of the harvests, of the effects of the storms upon the country; he writes of travellers in distant places, of the perils they run. He himself had been a mighty traveller, always at work, always in danger, but he rarely mentions the things he has accomplished or the things he still has in contemplation: it was not, indeed, till after his death that some of these latter bore fruit, that recommendations he had made were carried out, and his daughter enabled to edit and complete some of his unfinished labours.

When I myself was a girl my father told me that in his early married days no one was more hospitable to him and to my mother than a certain old lady—a cousin of his father's—living in Wimpole Street, where I can also remember her. This lady, Major Rennell's daughter, the beautiful Jane of whom her father was so proud, was the mother of little James. When my sister and I were children in Kensington, Lady Rodd's big carriage used to come driving up Young Street. We used to be taken for drives in it. I remember the grey lining, and the loops swaying and the tassels, and how this huge chariot used to swing and creak as it went along, while the kind old occupant talked of her own youth and her Admiral and of her son and of her grandchildren. On other occasions the ancient lady, with the dark eyes and the black old-fashioned hair, used to send for us to the carriage door, and she would then produce gifts, of rare make and dazzling hue, both Eastern and English too, and hand them out liberally. She was very fond of my father, and to the last he used to take us to call upon her.

It was, as I have said, between the years 1812–1827 that Major James Rennell was writing to his little grandson, and the boy's own grandchildren may now in turn look for themselves at the gentle, merry messages sent from Nassau Street, to the child in Cornwall, to the schoolboy at Temple Grove, to the more dignified Etonian; messages from the eighteenth to the nineteenth century and after!

"I am glad that you liked my letter, so I send you another," writes grandpapa, who seems to be for the moment staying in James's home. "Alicia says 'my love and a kiss.'" (Nursery talk has not changed much in the century which has passed since this correspondence began.) Then the epistle continues: "I hear that you ride on a man's saddle and that you play in the garden at Uncle Tremayne's."

As we read on, grandpapa seems to have returned to his own house. "I send you another red letter," he says; "I am much obliged to you for all your kindness to me whilst I was with you. I walked with your favourite Juno, in Portland Place this morning, and we talked about you."

James the Less at East Sheen received visits as well as letters.

"I do not know when I have enjoyed so heartfelt a sight [writes the grandfather to his grandson at Dr. Pinkney's, Temple Grove, East Sheen] as on the other day when we walked round the lawn and saw so many fine and promising young gentlemen engaged in innocent play. I have thought of it and mentioned it several times since, and consequently I have derived much comfort and have anticipated great advantages to yourself from all that I saw. . . ."

Collingwood's letters to his home are not more charming than the happy flow from the old warrior; remembering things for little James to remember.

"I hope the evening turned out fine on Wednesday [he writes on August 13, 1825], and that the Poney carried you pleasantly. The Duke's Park (Woburn) seems made for you and your Poney, and I should myself enjoy a ride of that kind. The Mansion House or Abbey seemed to me to be the least interesting part of the whole, but the Park, altogether, and particularly the *Green Lane*, delighted me.

"Saturday, yesterday, was a remarkably fine day, and I had some good walks. Your sisters were here and drank coffee with me. They sent several kisses which you may distribute. To-day, at half-past eight it began to rain, and I fear it will be a rainy day, but I shall watch the weather. The streets are black with people in mourning. I think I never saw shopping business so dull, or so few gentlefolk's carriages in the streets. I have read a good deal in your book, but there are many mistakes which you should be apprised of not to be misled— Captain Brenton allows three millions and a half of negro slaves in the Southern States of

America—I mean the United States, where by the last census there were a million and a half and no more, he certainly does not read. I have heard nothing more of Colonel Thackeray. Pray give my kind love to papa and mamma, and kind regards to Lady Inglis and the young ladies.—Your affectionate,

"G.-P. J. RENNELL."

"MY DEAR JAMES,—

. . . . . .

"You were in all your glory when in the pew with Mrs. Pinkney. I can remember things similar to it when I was a boy. I gave your kind messages to your sisters, and they send you their loves in return. I suppose that you know that our globe (earth) is flatted a little at the poles, and rises higher at the equator, and although the difference be only about 35 miles, yet it occasions vast changes in course of time, and in the going of a clock which may keep exact time here. If my clock was carried to any place near the equator, it would lose two minutes and a half per day. Jupiter is much flatter than our earth; one may perceive it in a large telescope.

"Did you hear that Dr. Oudeney and another gentleman with him exploring the interior of Africa are dead? These make twelve gentlemen who have been sent to explore Africa, and not one of them finally returned. Park came back the first time[1] and perished in the second. There are still two gentlemen alive of Dr. Oudeney's party who are pursuing their inquiries. My respects to Dr. and Mrs. Pinkney, and I hope you will favour me with another letter.—Your affectionate,

"G.-P. J. Rennell."

[1] It was Major Rennell who, having first constructed the map of the northern part of Africa in 1790, afterwards worked upon the notes and memoranda brought back by Mungo Park. Readers of Lockhart will remember Park's meetings with Walter Scott. "Calling one day at Fowlsheils and not finding Park at home, Scott walked in search of him along the banks of the Yarrow, which in that neighbourhood passes over various ledges of rock forming deep pools and eddies between them. Presently he discovered his friend standing alone on the bank plunging one stone after another into the water and watching anxiously the bubbles as they rose to the surface. 'This,' said Scott, 'appears but an idle amusement for one who has seen so much stirring adventure.' 'Not so idle perhaps as you suppose,' answered Mungo. 'This was the manner in which I used to ascertain the depth of a river in Africa before I ventured to cross it—judging whether the attempt would be safe by the time the bubbles of air took to ascend.' At this time Park's intention of a second expedition had never been revealed to Scott, but he instantly formed the opinion that these experiments on the Yarrow were connected with some such purpose."

Then again: "I had a letter from your good mamma two days ago; both she and your papa are very well at Rose Hill, Lord Northesk's place. They had a pleasant journey, and a fine walk in Farnham Park." Farnham Park is the ordinary residence of the Bishop of Winchester; Dean Rennell was his domestic chaplain, and lived there with Bishop Thomas.

"The corn was all down between this and Winchester. If the weather is fine next Wednesday, I propose to myself the happiness of seeing you. Your sisters are all well, and Alicia and Fanny send their love; so would Wilhelmina if she could speak, but though she cannot she makes herself understood. I suppose she must wonder why she cannot speak as well as everyone around her. I shall be very happy when your papa and mamma return, for that will be the signal for your speedy appearance. When you come I have a present for you to make to your good mamma. —Your affectionate,   G.-P. J. RENNELL."

One can almost see the little party reunited: James the Minor, the schoolboy, who must have been tall for his age, the grandfather not very tall, but gracefully built, as Walckenaer describes him, active and alert, with that gracious expressive head which is recorded by the medallion in the Abbey. One can picture them talking as they advance: the dog Juno following in their steps, as is the way with faithful dogs; the grandfather is telling the boy such facts as should interest him, telling him of adventures and experiences, perhaps of leopards and natural history, perhaps of Captain Parry's later exploits. They turn from Portland Place into Nassau Street, where Major Rennell lived on for so long a time, where his faithful old friends gathered round him year after year, and where his daughter and his son-in-law never failed to visit him sometimes twice a day, as he says.

The writer can remember James, a tall, fair, handsome man, very simple and unaffected, in turn absorbed in his own little boy—who, it may be mentioned, is now an ambassador and doing credit to his parentage.

The letters, after various holiday excursions into Bedfordshire and elsewhere, finally reach Eton itself:

"I hope you will find great pleasure in seeing

the Montem. It must really be a fine show.
So many youths together form a most delightful
spectacle to feeling minds. I am always affected
when I see a procession of charity boys and girls,
thinking what a vast promise there is to the next
generation.

"I hope the watch will arrive in good health"
(adds the kind grandpapa).

The letters give the news of those days; how
present some of it still is, and what familiar
names occur. Major Rennell was naturally in
touch with others of his kin. Every scientific
man of distinction came to him from abroad with
letters, from Humboldt and others, while over
here Sir Joseph Banks, Sir Hugh Inglis, Lord
Spencer, Sir Francis Beaufort, were his old personal friends, as well as all the Arctic travellers.

Apropos of Arctic exploration in 1824 he
writes :

" Your mamma will tell you a fine entertainment
Captain Parry gave on board the *Hecla*, and the
weather proved very indulgent, so that it went
off very well. Captain Parry and his companions, Captain Lyon and Captain Hoppner,
will return to the ice very soon. Captain Frank-

lin does not go yet awhile. What terrible hardships they must be prepared to encounter."

Again, later on: "The Russians have certainly failed in their plan of getting possession of Constantinople this time; so much the better for Europe. Although the Turks are sad dogs in comparison with the European nations at large, yet Europe would suffer by having the Russians in their places. Of two evils we should always choose the least."

Another letter comments upon a visit little James has lately paid to Richmond Hill.

" Richmond from whose front are eyed,
   Vale, spires, meandering streams and Windsor's tow'ry pride."

So Major Rennell quotes from Mr. Pope. He also remembers that Lord Palmerston once said "it was the employment of the gentlemen who lived at Richmond to drive to London and back again."

In February 1826 Major Rennell is writing of James's birthday:

"Years roll on [he says], and thus it comes round again to your birthday, and as I have no opportunity of embracing you, I can only convey to you in this way my congratulations. May these anniversaries return and find you as at present in the esteem of your friends, while the Almighty Ruler of all things shall vouchsafe to you the possession of your faculties.

"Your birthday will be kept at Easter when the Bird will fly in as usual, and summon you to Dinner; of which, I trust, I shall be able to partake. You know that other great Folks keep their Birthdays, not on the days on which they were born, but on some other—perhaps their *Name Day*, as is the custom on the Continent. I was telling your good Papa, that in such a case, yours must be kept on the 1st May, or the 25th July (for those are the days of the St. Jameses in the Calendar), and St. James *the Less* (the 1st May) ought to be *your* day; but then he has St. Philip quartered on him, and you would not give twopence for a *half* Birthday. Again, the 25th July is a long way off; and perhaps I ought to claim that Day for myself, as *that* St. James, the Son of Zebedee, is called St. James the *Major!*

"I was surprised to see how Mina was grown, and to feel her weight. I think Alicia and Fanny are much improved also. Mina said at Brighton that she should like to see me, and then return to Brighton.

"I forgot to write your Name in the Book of Maps. You had better write it on the inside of the Cover, as the Maps will not bear ink. I shall send you two Notes to stick into the Book.

"I went out with your Papa and Mamma yesterday, for the first time of going out since the day on which you returned to Eton, 14th January.

"Believe me, my dearest James,—Your affectionate Grandpapa,   J. RENNELL.

"28*th February* 1826."

Again: "MY DEAREST JAMES,—I have received your very kind letters, three in number, all of which gave me much pleasure as far as concerned yourself, but I confess I felt it very awful in what related to your neighbours. These explosive storms, I conclude, are part of the system by which the purity of the atmosphere is upheld. When a boy I was much alarmed at lightning, but being at length compelled by duty to face it in company with a number of others, I became so accustomed to it that by degrees it grew to be an amusement to observe the different *kinds* of lightning. Do you know that sometimes lightning strikes from the ground to the clouds —at others and more commonly the contrary; often from one cloud to another, but never reciprocally. Once a mass of it passed so near to me that I plainly smelt it; it smelt like red-hot iron and made a whizzing noise like a cannon ball.

"The gout still plagues me so that I cannot walk as usual; what your presence may effect I know not, but what I possess is at your service. —Your affectionate Grandpapa, J. RENNELL.

"1st *July* 1826."

In 1827 he says: "I suppose you hear something about our Thames Tunnel. It has lately lost its way and got into the River. It is, however, no joking concern to subscribers, who will suffer a great loss; I believe they did not leave a sufficient thickness of ground between the tunnel and the bottom of the River. I always regarded it as a wild sort of plan. . . .

"I am afraid Mr. Canning's health is on the decline, the cessation of his Parliamentary Duties will afford him much relief.

"I remain, my dear James,—Your very affectionate G.-P., J. RENNELL."

The shades are beginning to close in, but he writes still cheerfully on the 19th of June 1827:

"MY DEAR JAMES,—I have long been your debtor, for want of being able to pay you. Three of your very kind letters now lie before me as if reproaching me for my neglecting them. The truth is, that my right hand has suffered very much (the left still more), and for a long time it was very painful to use the finger and thumb, nor have I been able to walk across the room. My friends, however, do not desert me, for I seldom miss having company every day, and very commonly ladies. Your Papa and Mamma I see every day, and sometimes more than once, your sisters also . . . but I cannot return any of their visits. 20*th*.—Your sister Alicia came home yesterday. She is wonderfully tall, and looks very well. You remember Lord Abercorn's shrubbery—'*Nothing to do, but to grow.*'

"I congratulate you on your accession to the Fifth Form. Martin Thackeray was expatiating on the subject."

II

These extracts speak for themselves, but before ending this little paper it is meet to dwell for a moment not only on James's grandfather, but on the Major himself in his long and gallant career and life of faithful work, inspired by that natural genius for observation which was his own. From his early youth to his gentle old age, this wise and charming philosopher never ceased to follow the gleam as it shone for him.

Baron Walckenaer, as Secretary of the Institute of France, wrote a fine tribute to "Jacques Rennell" (so he calls him), who for thirty years had been associated as a member of the Institute.

"The hydrographical problems which young Rennell grasped presented special difficulties [says the Baron]. In order to triumph over them it was necessary to join to Knowledge and to Practice, Patience, Courage, Presence of Mind, none of which could be allowed to relax for a single instant during the course of the operations. It is necessary in such experiments as his, to consult almost simultaneously the earth, the heavens and the sea, to add the movements of the planets to those horizons, of which the sinuosities, the heights and the aspects are being measured. When the problems concern the moving and capricious surface of the waters, the level must be measured every quarter of an hour; and you have to concert measures with other observers on the shore, besides sounding the depths of the sea. Some of these observations, wearying and often accompanied by danger, have to be repeated twenty, forty times, if one wishes to avoid errors, of which the slightest might occasion such serious disaster. . . ."

Baron Walckenaer writes no less sympathetically of the end than of the beginning of this fine career. "Long after the Major had been obliged by the state of his health to give up all society, a certain number of friends still came to visit him at fixed hours, sitting with him by the large table where lay spread the maps, the compasses, the books necessary for the work upon which he was engaged. When the conversation fell upon subjects upon which he was an authority, he had an art all his own of inculcating his facts with so much simplicity and clearness that people seemed to remember that which he was teaching them at the time."

Titles and recognition were less common in the 1700's than they are now, but, nevertheless, respect and admiration existed then as happily they do still. I happened once, when he was over here not long ago, to mention Major Rennell's name to Major Sykes, H.M. Consul-General in Persia (well known himself for his work and varied attainments), and he burst out in warm and vivid praise of one whose teaching, he said, he had followed all his life with an ever-increasing respect.

"Undoubtedly the first great English geographer," says Sir Clements Markham, writing of Major Rennell in the "Century Science" series.

Sir Edward Thackeray, in his *Biographies of the Royal Bengal Engineers*, gives this story of Major Rennell. He says of him:

"Among his eager fortune-seeking countrymen, Major Rennell stands forth as a unique figure—a calm, disinterested man of science. When the Peace of Paris in 1763 seemed to end his chances in the British Navy, he received an ensign's commission in the Bengal Engineers, and was appointed surveyor of the Company's dominions in Bengal, and during these years some of his most eventful experiences befell him."

Major Rennell's own account of one of his experiences with the "Facqueers," as he calls them, is well worth quoting at length. He was reconnoitring the country on the borders of Bhutan at the time. (How often little James must have asked for the story which his grandfather tells in a letter to a friend.)

"Suddenly we found ourselves in front of two lines of 'Facqueers' drawn up in the market-place [so he writes in August 1766]. Our escort found it high time to retreat, but we thought it rather too late, for the enemy had drawn their swords and surrounded us. One of the officers escaped unhurt, the other with a slight wound after fighting his way through. As for myself I was so entirely surrounded that I never expected to escape, but having the good fortune to preserve my sword, I defended myself pretty well in front and kept retreating backwards till I had very few behind me when I turned and fled for it. A hardy fellow followed me close, but paid the price of his life; the rest of them thinking me too much wounded to run far, remained in their places, but kept a continual firing on me till I was out of sight. Providence must have strengthened my arms while I was retreating, for now I found both of them deprived of their strength. Indeed, no wonder, one of them was cut in three places, and the shoulder-bone belonging to the other divided. One stroke of a sabre had cut my right shoulder-bone through, and laid me open for nearly a foot, besides a large cut in the hand, which has deprived me of the use of my forefinger. . . ."

For surgical aid Rennell had to be sent to Dacca, three hundred miles off, in an open boat, which he had to direct himself, as he lay upon his face, while the natives applied onions as cataplasm to the wounds. He was long given up, but under the care of Dr. Russell recovered, though his health was seriously shaken by the loss of blood and severity of the wounds.

Among many subsequent adventures, we are told of him one day "marching in India at the head of a detachment," and as we read in the *European Magazine*, " he was suddenly attacked by a 'tyger.' With great coolness he received the animal on the point of the bayonet, which he thrust down his throat and so despatched him, but it appears that the bayonet was much bent."

The Major's own account of the affair makes the "tyger" into a leopard—"Five of my men were wounded by him, four very dangerously. You see I am a lucky fellow at all times," says he.

It was in the year 1772, after the fight with the "Facqueers," that Major Rennell was married to Miss Jane Thackeray, my father's great-aunt. There is a family tradition, which I may be allowed to mention, that when this young lady departed from her home to stay in Bengal with her youngest brother, the W. M. Thackeray of those days, Mrs. Thackeray, the experienced mother of sixteen, exclaimed: "If there is a sensible man in all India he will find out our Jenny."

Jenny and her beautiful younger sister

Henrietta had started for India at the invitation of their youngest brother, the original William Makepeace Thackeray, my father's namesake and grandfather, a *protégé* of Mr. Cartier, the Lieutenant-Governor of Bengal. It was at Mr. Cartier's house that the Thackerays made the acquaintance of "the sensible man," so we read in the *History of the Thackerays in India*.

The marriage was a happy one; but some years after, Major Rennell's health having failed from the hardships he had gone through, the couple came back to England. Both their sons died comparatively young, but the daughter Jane remained to them. She married a naval captain, afterwards Admiral Sir John Tremayne Rodd, and, as I have said, was the mother of little James, to whom the letters are addressed. Old friends used to say how proud Major Rennell was of his daughter's beauty and abilities, and she herself has related that her father had said to her : "You may always rely on your own judgment *if it is on a subject you understand;* if not, take advice." She was thus able to edit some of his unfinished writings after his death.

Mrs. Rennell died first; Major Rennell lived

on till he was over 87 in his quiet retreat with the faithful old housekeeper. As we have seen, his grandchildren, his old friends, his daughter and his son-in-law, never left him long alone.

This is an age of pictures. There are few people who do not love them. Besides the actual representations of things that we see with our eyes, and the images of the benefactors we have actually known, there are also those pictures which we paint for ourselves, memory-pictures, hope-pictures, wishing-pictures, all depicted upon that mysterious atmosphere which surrounds our life as it passes. It sometimes happens that these visions show us men and women who never knew us, who died long before we were born, and yet who are actually a part of our lives and in some way still with us and full of help and sympathy, and encouragement. Major Rennell is one of these; he had a personal charm for his contemporaries, as he has had for many of those who have followed. His daughter, his grandson, and his grandson's wife ever retained a devoted affection for his memory.

"Rennell was of medium height, well proportioned, of a grave yet sweet expression of countenance. The miniature painted for Lord Spencer represents him sitting in his arm-chair as in reflection. He was diffident and unassuming, but ever ready to impart information." So writes Sir Clements Markham in the *Dictionary of National Biography*, that *Campo Santo* where the honoured names of those who have done well for their country are recorded.

After Major Rennell's death, when he was laid to his rest in Westminster Abbey on April 6, 1830, the old friends who had come so faithfully, and with so much regard, to the little house in Nassau Street, put up a medallion to his memory. It is at the entrance of Poet's Corner—it depicts a refined and charming head with the old-fashioned collar and tie wig of the period; I can see in it some look of my old benefactress as I look at it, and of one of her grandchildren. The hand of that erratic sculptor, Nature, gives us from time to time glimpses of those who have lived, whose children and grandchildren look at us still with their eyes and speak to us with their voices.

MORLAND AT FRESHWATER BAY

I

It is with a delightful response that one comes upon Morland's well-known picture of "The Stable" in the National Gallery. I was actually searching for it when my admiration was arrested by a vision of harmonious, tranquil life. A peaceful gleam rather than a picture met my gaze, and as I looked I realised that this was what I was seeking. All in it is natural, inevitable, as the greatest and best must always seem.

The day is ending; the horses and the pony are led home, contentedly returning from their toil. The stableman stoops to collect the provender; the light flows in, shaded from without by the piece of irradiated sacking, and as it illumines the homely things—the wheelbarrow, the spade, the old lantern—these very implements seem also at rest. Toil is over; the hour of peace has come.

MORLAND AT FRESHWATER BAY

There are other fine pictures by Morland, but nothing seems quite so good as this one, which, so I have been told, was bought and presented to the nation by a generous benefactor. But though nothing is perhaps quite equal to "The Stable," one is dazzled by the wealth of the stream which comes flowing from the easel of this ardent workman. Sometimes one is disappointed in his work, which seems to have been alternately a torrent of realisation, of vitality, and a drifting waste of fine material.

In his early youth horses were his delight; he rode in steeplechases. He was a fine musician as well as a painter; he was a gay and generous companion, a happy vagrant all through life, spending recklessly, giving out bountifully to the end. He might have claimed a baronetcy, but he refused, and said, "Better be a fine painter than a fine gentleman."

George Morland was born in 1764. He was the son of Henry Morland, also an artist, from whom he received whatever tuition he had in drawing and painting. We read how, as a boy, he was made to work so hard that when he reached manhood he went to the opposite extreme, and his life was wild, amusing, and agreeable. He married the sister of William Ward, the mezzotint engraver (who reproduced so many of his pictures). Morland loved his wife, but after a short time of married life, grew tired of domestic monotony, quarrelled with his brother-in-law, and once more returned to Bohemian ways. His health broke down; he owed money, and was imprisoned for debt. One of his pictures is a scene representing a half-naked prisoner being relieved by two kind benefactors.

Morland fled from debts and bailiffs—perhaps he rather enjoyed flying from his creditors—and finally came to the Isle of Wight and painted many of its aspects.

There is that wonderful episode related in his life when, being at breakfast at six o'clock in the morning at Yarmouth in the island, preparing for his day's work, a corporal and a file of soldiers marched in and took him off to Newport as a spy, wearily trudging him through the blazing sun. Happily one of the magistrates set him free, and from Yarmouth and Newport he seems to have found his way to Freshwater Bay.

Coming out of Farringford Lane, where the thrushes still sing as they did in the laureate's time, and the downs shine beyond the fragrant hedges, you pass between them, still following the road to the foot of the hill, where one or two patient loiterers stand watching the passers-by; finally, you come to a little sea-terrace marked by a few posts and chains. Perhaps as you look about a gull sails by on tranquil extended pinions, you see a few bathing-machines huddled among the waste and lumber of the shore, and on the opposite cliff a long low inn of only two stories marked by a flagstaff. It is now called the Albion. A hundred years ago a little public-house, the Mermaid, stood on the self-same spot; it was a very humble Mermaid and a place of meeting, so we are told, for smugglers and fishermen. It is in full range of the broad sea-breezes; on stormy days the waves still come from a great distance, sending sudden fountains of spray against the low windows. The Stag rocks are opposite; on the other side, the fort half-way up the cliff leads to High Down and to its beacon wrapped in changing lights. Gulls fly across the line of the cliff, countless rabbits scamper along the turf. The ancient wooden beacon has been replaced by Tennyson's cross, but nothing else is very different from the time —a hundred years ago—when George Morland looked out with his flashing dark eyes and saw it all. Here in little Freshwater he lived for a time and worked and joined the wild revellers who then frequented the humble tavern. There is the story of the friend who reproached him for keeping such humble company and dragged him reluctantly away from the bar. But once outside, Morland produced his sketch-book. "Look at this," said he; "where else could I find such models?" and there were the admirable drawings of the men drinking within.

"George Morland," says Mr. Richardson, "the successor of Reynolds and Romney, of Hogarth, of Gainsborough, was, like Burns, absolutely original, averse to seeking knowledge in any academy but that of nature."

In Mr. Wedmore's *Studies in English Art*, writing of landscape, he says: "Gainsborough had discovered a mine which others would more profitably work. He had set an example, and others would follow it, though the result of their following would vary with their individual gifts. Two men who worked in part during his later life, and in chief after its close, I connect especially with Gainsborough. The art of each had a new element, but the art of both was the child of Gainsborough. One of these men was George Morland; the other, Francis Wheatley."

To go on quoting from Mr. Wedmore: "To high dramatic expression Morland did not seek to attain; to subtle and fine feeling he hardly pretended; but unconcerned with the modern landscapist's philosophy, or any wider vision than that which lay before his own peasant as he trudged home from his work, or his own fisherman as he mended the nets on the beach, or his own shepherd as he paused at midday to take from his wallet his meal, while the good dogs barked around him—unconcerned with any wider vision than that of these, Morland did slowly build up for us a picture of the rougher England of that day."

Many of Morland's prints and drawings are still to be found in the island. From the cottages they have gradually drifted to the halls and homes of the well-to-do. Mrs. Orchard at the Freshwater Post Office has a charming collection of Morland's sketches as well as some of those of his colleagues and imitators.

Among her prints is one called "The Fern Gatherers," a print after Morland, published in 1799, $17\frac{1}{2}$ by $23\frac{3}{4}$. It is curious as being the original of a charming duplicate in water colour by Ward. The water colour has also been engraved, and is called "The Fern Burners." In it only a part of the first picture is repeated. The figure of a gipsy is altogether omitted, and the position of another slightly altered. The plate of this "Fern Burners" has been destroyed.

II

It is a long way from Freshwater Gate to Queen Anne's Gate at the Westminster end of St. James's Park, where in a stately old mansion traces of Morland's life-work are also to be found—early and fanciful studies in his finished early style, so unlike his broader later manner: "Idleness," the tranquil lady in white attire with her little dog to keep her company; "Industry," the most charming and leisurely of industries, with her broad black hat so deftly poised upon her elaborate locks and with pretty red slippers resting on a footstool. She delicately stitches at arm's length while the light falls upon her sampler. In the hall of the same old house the well-known children playing at soldiers are to be seen, with that dear little girl in the foreground looking on. Still more delightful are those infants of the past robbing the orchard of long-stolen apples. They are dressed in ancient little knee-breeches and shoe-buckles. For a century past the little scapegrace has come scrambling from the branches, while another clutches at the fallen fruit. It is all delicate, natural; at the same time we may realise Morland's great advance as time went on. At the Victoria and Albert Museum I found one picture which appealed to me, that of the fishermen hauling in a boat from the sea. I thought I could recognise the very place in Freshwater Bay. The waves of the sea are alive, the clouds are alive, the dog is alive, even the cliffs are alive in their own fashion; only the fishermen are not alive as they haul in the boat, though the craft is yielding to their pull and the wind blows their hair and their clothing.

His anatomy may have failed somewhat, but he could paint time, he could paint rest, he could paint the essence of life, and his wayward attraction, strange being that he was, adds something not to be ignored to its realisation. With so many selves to enjoy, with so many qualities to squander, his music, his riding, his love of animals, his love of children, his jovial charity, his prodigal companionship, he should have been a greater man. Morland as he grew older took a wider view of life and nature than in his youth. He must have been a lovable person. His wife died of grief when she learnt his death. She owed him love; we owe to him a new delight in natural things.

How often it is the thought of the others who have passed before us that gives a personal soul and meaning to nature itself.

Freshwater, where Morland once came, has its own beloved traditions, traditions greater than Morland's, and coming after him, and it echoes with the footsteps which still seem to be crossing the downs and treading the lanes and the meadows all around.

[1] A friend shows me this cutting from *The Athenæum*, April 26, 1913: "Engravings after Morland fetched the following prices: 'The Story of Letitia,' by J. R. Smith (set of six), £861; 'A Visit to the Boarding School' and 'A Visit to the Child at Nurse,' by W. Ward (a pair), £420; 'Children Playing at Soldiers,' £231."

ALFRED STEVENS

A SHRINE on the Westminster Embankment, no less sacred to Art than those classic monuments dedicated to Apollo and the Muses, or that lovely temple of Venus which is still standing by the flowing Tiber, is happily to be seen any day by the passer-by reflected in the waters of the Thames; flights of easy steps lead up to the open portals, inviting and open to all. But a few days ago the votaries were assembling in numbers to testify their devout gratitude for the gifts of beauty and expression which are to be found in the Tate Gallery, and of which every day brings more and more interesting examples. On this special occasion, Lord Plymouth opened the proceedings by introducing Sir William Richmond, who made the presentation of the bust of Alfred Stevens by Professor Lantéri, and the fine model of mouldings from Holford House; paying generous tribute to To-day as well as to Yesterday, and to

Stevens's "indomitable will and commanding love for all forms of artistic expression." . . . "Fashions were fugitive, he said, but great art was eternal." . . . Among those who listened to this voice, and to others which so fitly followed, was the President of the "Alfred Stevens Memorial Committee," M. Alphonse Legros, warmly and enthusiastically welcomed by the younger men, as he slowly advanced to the front bearing with dignity all the weight of his honoured years. It was a moment not to be forgotten; the old man entered the hall, the younger generation rose to receive him, advancing with outstretched hands and eager response to lead him to his chair. It was Legros's last public appearance, and the legitimate satisfaction of his long and generous desire for the recognition of Stevens's genius.

We cannot do better than quote a few sentences from the introductory note to the Catalogue of the Alfred Stevens's Loan Collection at the Tate Gallery, opened on the 15th of November 1911:

"It had long been the desire of Professor Legros that a monument to Stevens should find a place in the Gallery of British Art. The memorial committee was formed under his presidency, and raised the funds necessary to add the reproduction of the chimney-piece to the memorial bust; these now take their place in what will be for the future a Stevens's room.

"The design for the completed monument of the Duke of Wellington is to be seen at the South Kensington Museum, 'with the equestrian statue,' as the Catalogue tells us, 'ruled out by a caprice of the Dean.'"

Some work seems complete in its moment, other seems to belong to that "eternal world of great Art"; and as we look at the drawings and noble designs which are left to us by Alfred Stevens, this man of yesterday, who died too early to reap the recognition of his genius, we are carried back to Michael Angelo, to Leonardo, to the mighty powers of the past. Perhaps our generation is in some measure better able to appreciate great work than many of those which immediately preceded it. It is certainly not behindhand in giving Stevens his due.

When the seeding time at last comes round, thoughts are scattered and carried far afield;

names seem to be in the air. Of late the name of Alfred Stevens has echoed from every side, conjured out of the silence. Sculptor, painter, decorator, he was an artist in the largest, truest sense, a lifelong follower of truth and beauty.

He was born in 1818 at Blandford Fordham, in Dorsetshire. His father was a house-painter who practised the collateral trades or branches of decoration, sign-painting and heraldic work. The elder Stevens was considered a clever man by his neighbours; some of them were still alive when Mr. Stannus visited the town about eighteen years ago. Alfred worked with his father from the age of eleven to fifteen. Then the Rector of an adjacent village, who greatly admired his gifts, gave fifty pounds towards his education as a painter, and it was agreed that he should be sent to study in London. The boy evinced a vocation for drawing animals, and Sir Edwin Landseer was chosen as a suitable master, but, happily for Stevens's career, Sir Edwin did not take pupils under five hundred pounds—a far larger sum than was forthcoming—it was therefore settled that the young student should go to Italy and there prepare himself for an artistic career.

A portrait of Alfred Stevens, designed by himself about this time, is very delightful. The boy looks out from the page with intelligent brown eyes, he wears his thick brown hair somewhat long; his expression is already full of character and determination, the strong personality impresses itself as one looks at it; a painter is always the best depictor of himself.

The author of *Erewhon* says somewhere: "A great portrait is always more a portrait of the painter than of the painted. When we look at a portrait by Holbein or Rembrandt, it is of Holbein or Rembrandt we think, more than of the subject of their pictures. Even a portrait of Shakespeare by Holbein or Rembrandt could tell us very little about Shakespeare. It would, however, tell us a great deal about Holbein or Rembrandt." This seems to apply especially to Stevens and his work, and to this boyish portrait from which one undoubtedly learns a great deal of the man-to-be.

Alfred Stevens arrived at Naples in October 1833; he had sixty pounds in his pocket, much good advice from his friends, and special injunctions that he was to study the works of Salvator Rosa, who at that time was very much the fashion; but he rejected Salvator, and instead of following the conventional path, he struck out an entirely original one of his own devising, and worked hard at it making studies from the works of Giotto, and copying any of the pictures of Andrea del Sarto that he found in the Galleries. The excavations of Pompeii were just then in full progress, and we find an exquisite little water-colour in the Tate Gallery which is described in the Catalogue as "A study of a street in Pompeii, with touches of colour, showing the source of much of Stevens's inspiration in decoration." "A study of a purple single peony, an early work," hangs above it, a lovely, delicate drawing of a peony flowering, nearly a hundred years ago, and not to be forgotten. In the same room we find two striking oil pictures; one is the portrait of a young man, the other evidently that of an artist. The smaller picture represents a painter sitting in a perfectly bare room or studio; it is carpetless, paperless, the walls are grey and discoloured, a black stove is the only ornament; there is also a shabby doorway to be seen, stained by time. But the emptiness is not empty, the bareness is not bare, the light is there shining from those walls of luminous grey. One is arrested by the delicate, expressive face. There are no adjuncts, except truth indeed and life. The dress is that of the early Victorian time, the high-collared coat, the black neck-tie tied in a heavy bow, the hair not cropped as now, but allowed to grow: it all arrests you, no less than did the picturesque figures who once worked (as they still do) in artistic garb, who wore fur for their painter's livery, broad hats like Rubens and Vandyke. It may, to some of us, be a new lesson to realise that art is to be found everywhere, not in beautiful things only, but in plain and obvious ones, in reserve as well as in superfluity. As an instance of the value of the homely in a kindred art may we not quote the works of Hardy and Meredith.

When Stevens left Naples at last it was on foot, and he slowly made his way to Rome, putting up at night in the wayside inns, where in order to pay for his lodging and food he sold pencil portraits brushed over with colour. He led the strenuous life of a painter of old, he travelled from place to place, always observing, always learning and improving. Finally, he came to Florence, where he stayed for three years, and we are told that his aptitude for anatomy was such that his teacher advised him to take to surgery and to give up art. But art was the breath of life to him.

His sixty pounds were long since exhausted; he kept himself by selling copies of the old masters to the dealers. He entered so entirely into the feeling of the original pictures that when in later days he exhibited some of his copies at the Royal Academy many people insisted they could not be his, but must have been old pictures which he had purchased on the spot.

In 1839 Stevens was at Milan studying ornament under Albertolli, and in spare moments measuring the fronts of the palaces. He returned to Rome in 1840, where, to gain a living, he became clerk of works to a builder, in which position he was most unpopular, owing to the amount of work he exacted from the men. After this, he became acquainted with Thorwaldsen, the sculptor, of whom Mr. Stannus tells us he often spoke with gratitude, and declared that he was the only man to whom he owed any pupilage.

In 1842, after fourteen years of unceasing study, Stevens at last returned to England, perhaps the most thoroughly educated artist the country has ever seen. He had never worked in any English school; his entire training was acquired in Italy. Then he went back to his home in Dorsetshire, where he remained for a year or two, unappreciated and misunderstood—not an uncommon experience.

The following little story, which Mr. Stannus quotes as being typical of Stevens, should belong to this time. A musical friend of his was trying to make an ophicleide for use in an amateur band, and having finished the straight pipe, could get no further. Stevens thereupon came to the rescue, cut out the shapes of the brass sheets in brown paper, and these plates when bent and hammered up served perfectly for the desired purpose. This feat became the talk of the town, and Stevens was spoken of "as the young man who could not only paint pictures that were of no use to any one, but could also make brass instruments which could play music."

In 1845, when he was twenty-seven years of age, he was appointed to a post in the Government School of Design, and he writes to a friend: "I was sent for the other day to Somerset House and offered a place in the School of Design as Professor of everything. The place is one which will at once put me in such an excellent position, and is so well fitted for me, that I expect to gain much credit by it. I don't think I can expect too much from it. The salary will make me quite independent. It interferes scarcely at all with my time. . . . I got this place without any sort of interest, and without solicitation on my own part."

We read that Stevens made himself generally beloved and appreciated; his pupils were delighted with him. He had a quick, piercing eye, a most winning smile, and the sweetness of his voice and manner had great influence over them all. Stannus tells us that the young master's powerful, dexterous brush-work created a sensation among the students.

There is a little story of how Richard Beavis,

afterwards very well known, who was working under him, said on one occasion, "I sketched in the ornaments, sir." To which Stevens replied, "We don't sketch here, we draw." Ellis and Townroe, two of his pupils at this time, afterwards worked under him for the Wellington Memorial.

But after two years only Stevens resigned his appointment, "disgusted," he said in after days, "by the meddlesome supervision of ignorant Government clerks." Thus the school, losing his inspiration and decorative teaching, fell back into the Slough of Despond, until 1860, when Stevens's good influence revived through the teaching of his pupils, Sykes and others, who were masters at South Kensington under the enterprising management of Sir Henry Cole.

All this time Stevens had been doing a great deal of book illustration, drawing pictures for the Bible, for Shakespeare, and Homer. He also sent in designs for Macaulay's *Lays of Ancient Rome*, but Macaulay preferred the style of Scharf. Whatever Stevens took in hand he seemed to illuminate with his gift. There is no end to the things which he achieved. Deysbrook, a manor near Liverpool, belonging to the Blundell family, was entirely decorated by him. The lovely drawings for the work are to be seen in the South Kensington Museum. He also took in hand a house in Palace Gardens, belonging to the Murietta family. He was so rapid a worker that only a fortnight was required for the Deysbrook drawings, and we are told that Stevens executed them without a model. It is almost bewildering to follow the many impressions of his mind. Among other things, military uniforms occupied his attention; then came a design for a royal railway carriage, like a fairy chariot, for the King of Denmark. The King was so pleased that he begged the artist to come and settle in Denmark, but this offer Stevens refused.

In 1848 the improvement of the Nelson Column was under discussion, and Landseer's lions had not then been thought of. Stevens entered into the scheme; his idea was to give some refinement in scale to the pedestal, by the addition of figures and ornaments in bronze upon the hollow moulding. The original beautiful plaster sketch of the proposed addition is to be seen at South Kensington. In 1850 every British and Irish manufacturer of any note was straining his utmost to prepare a worthy show in the great Exhibition which was to be held in the following year. Stevens, who had been engaged as manager by Messrs. Hoole & Co., seconded by his assistants, Godfrey Sykes and Townroe, produced a number of suggestions for homely use, such as hot-air stoves, &c. The firm carried away every medal in 1851, and outdistanced all competition. It is no exaggeration to say that his work caused a new development in bronze and iron. Stevens, without previous training, appears to have mastered the technical requirements from the first, while the æsthetic instinct taught him to design every adornment of the right kind in its right place. Before his time, our bronze and iron manufacturers had chiefly depended on rococo ornaments produced by second-rate foreigners.

On Saturday, September 13, 1856, the newspapers advertised for designs for the Wellington Memorial. A friend of Stevens hurried off to him with the information. By Monday morning he decided to compete. He was living at that time at 7 Canning Place, Kensington, and in the little back room he made the model for the monument, while the front room was occupied with his office drawings. The proposed position of the Wellington Monument, so we are told, fired his imagination. It is only now, thanks to Lord Leighton's efforts, which have been continued to this day by those who have eyes to see and influence to enforce, that the monument is to be seen where it was meant to be; and will be admired, noble and complete at last, and as Stevens saw it in his mind.

His fastidiousness in not parting with any work until the last moment nearly caused the miscarriage of the Wellington Memorial. The last day for sending it in was Whit Monday, and his friend Ellis spent the whole day seeking high and low for a cart to convey the model to Westminster Hall. At last, in the evening, he found a pleasure-van returning from Hampstead Heath, and into this the model was hoisted, and after the horses had rested the van started once more. Ellis accompanied it, and arrived at Westminster three minutes before midnight. After much persuasion, he got some workmen to help him carry it into the Hall, where it arrived just as the clock struck twelve.

Stevens's name came out only sixth in the list of competitors, but when the designs were tried under the model of the arch in St. Paul's, where they were to stand, his was found to be the only one suitable.

After this great effort he went to Italy once more to refresh his mind. He examined many monuments and churches there, and it is said on his return that, on going into his study and looking at his own design, he said, "Not so bad, after all."

The Catalogue of the National Gallery of British Art tells the story of the fortune bequeathed to him by a friend, an American, who admired his genius so much that he left him all he had; but when Stevens found there were relations who had counted on the money, he gave it back to them, only keeping two folios in which his friend had written his name. He had few companions. He shunned society; he lived for his work. I have been told of people trying in vain to make his acquaintance in the studio at Hampstead where he lived, and absolutely refused anyone admittance to his house.

Meanwhile the great monument, his utterance to the world, the noble tribute to the mighty warrior, was raised with its emblems, in its strength and beauty, its delicate and exquisite detail.

But there was still much to endure for a man of Stevens's sensitive nature. He was harassed by critics, hampered by the delay of payment to enable him to complete his work. In 1875 he wrote to Mr. Pegler, a lifelong friend, a letter which is a reply to some of those who had so greatly harassed him. In less than twelve hours after writing the letter he died quite suddenly. . . .

We are told that absence of material prevented any official memoir being written. But a richly illustrated and interesting folio volume was published in 1891 by the Autotype Company, in which the bare facts of the painter's life are to be found, with notes by his faithful pupil, Hugh Stannus. Stevens was neither given to letter-writing, nor to keeping a diary. It is in the mass of drawings and scribblings, and in the manifold studies he left, that his history is told. We see thought upon thought, impression upon impression, dawning from the first incoherence into completeness. Stevens cared for the beautiful, he scorned the material machinery of success and advancement; what he loved was Art; he worshipped at the shrine of beauty and power. With St. Peter, he could say, "Silver and gold have I none, but such as I have, give I thee."

A. R. AND H. R.

REMINISCENCES

P

CONCERNING THE FOUNDING OF THE "CORNHILL MAGAZINE"

WHAT we call, and what our children in turn will call, old days, are the days of our early youth, and to the writer the old days of the *Cornhill Magazine* convey an impression of early youth, of constant sunshine mysteriously associated with the dawn of the golden covers, even though it was in winter that they first appeared.

Recalling those vivid times, she cannot but think instinctively of the friends who also lived then, of her father and her home as it was then, of George Smith, the founder of the *Cornhill*, of his far-reaching life of generous achievement, of the companion of that life whose voice never unheeded, whose influence always counting for so much, was that of the tender wife and helpmate, to whom he ever turned, and his children with him.

Not many words are needed to speak of the jubilee of the *Cornhill* in 1910. There is nothing new to say, except that which happily is not new, and continues still to belong to its traditions; no less than in the days when its founder, the builder of so many great enterprises, first spoke of it to the first editor. Through the years which have followed, and when among others Leslie Stephen was editor in turn, that good tradition has not changed.

"Our magazine is written not only for men and women, but for boys, girls, infants," my father says.

And to add to this there is what each of us may remember for ourselves. What philosophies, what fine utterances have rung from the familiar shrine, and what honoured voices have echoed thence!

I am told that my father demurred at first to the suggestion of editing the *Cornhill*. Such work did not lie within his scope, but then Mr George Smith arranged that he himself was to undertake all business transactions, and my father was only to go on writing and criticising and suggesting; and so the first start of the *Cornhill* was all gaily settled and planned. The early records of the start still to be read of in

the old diaries, are of a cheerful character—
no time is lost—business questions are adjourned
to Greenwich, to dinners there, to gardens—
friendly meetings abound. . . .

I have an impression also, besides the play,
of very hard and continuous work during all
that time; of a stream of notes and messengers
from Messrs. Smith & Elder; of consultations,
calculations. I find an old record which states
that "in sixteen days" the *Cornhill* was planned
and equipped for its long journey.

My father would go to Wimbledon, where the
young couple Mr. and Mrs. George Smith were
then living. Later on it was Mr. Smith who
used to come and see my father, in Onslow
Square, driving in early, morning after morning,
on his way to business, carrying a certain black
bag full of papers and correspondence, and
generally arriving about breakfast-time.

On September 1, 1859, the following entry
occurs in Mr. George Smith's diary:

"*Went to dine at Greenwich with Thackeray
to talk about magazine.*"

On January 1, 1860 (only four months later),
the first number of the *Cornhill* was published.

We read, on January 3, 1860: "*Called on Thackeray on my way to the City; signed agreement respecting 'Roundabout Papers.' Mr. Thackeray in very good spirits at the success of the* Cornhill.

"January 27, 1860.—*No. 2 published—ordered* 80,000 *to be printed. Called in Bride Lane to see how they were selling the second number of the magazine. The demand very rapid.*

"January 30, 1860.—*Ordered* 100,000 *to be printed of* Cornhill Magazine.

"May 31, 1860.—*To Thackeray with first volume of magazine.*"

Mr. George Smith has himself told us of how the first idea of the magazine came to him. He says:

"The plan flashed upon me suddenly, as did most of the ideas which have in the course of my life led to successful operations. The existing magazines were few, and when not high-priced were narrow in literary range; and it seemed to me that a shilling magazine which contained, in addition to other first-class literary matter, a serial novel by Thackeray, must command a large sale. Thackeray's name was one to conjure with, and according to the plan, as it shaped itself in my mind, the public would have a serial novel by Thackeray, and a good deal else worth reading, for the price they had been accustomed to pay for the monthly number of his novels alone."

We know how successfully "the plan" worked, what a remarkable and willing army of helpers joined the enterprise.

Anthony Trollope, a stately herald, opened the first number of the *Cornhill* with his delightful history of *Framley Parsonage;* my father wound up with the "Roundabout Paper" called "On a Lazy Idle Boy," and he describes the magazine while addressing the young reader:

"Our *Cornhill Magazine* owners strive to provide thee with facts as well as fiction," he says, "and though it does not become them to brag of their ordinary, at least they invite thee to a table where thou shalt sit in good company."

Further on he writes concerning his own story, *Lovel the Widower* and *Framley Parsonage,* as of "Two novels under two flags; the one that ancient ensign which has hung before the well-known booth of 'Vanity Fair,' the other that fresh and handsome standard which has lately been hoisted on 'Barchester Towers.'"

Father Prout's beautiful inaugurative ode appeared in the first number. It is addressed to the author of *Vanity Fair:*

> "There's corn in Egypt still
>   (Pilgrim from Cairo to Cornhill!)
>   Give each his fill;
>   But all comers among
>   Treat best the young;
>   Fill the big brothers' knapsacks from thy bins,
>   But slip the Cup of Love in BENJAMIN'S...."

And the poem concludes with a grace almost sung to music:

> "Courage, old Friend! long found
>   Firm at thy task, not in fixt purpose fickle:
>   Up! choose thy ground,
>   Put forth thy shining sickle:
>   Shun the dense underwood
>   Of Dunce or Dunderhood:
>   But reap North, South, East, Far West,
>   The world-wide Harvest!"

The poet of the past sang of the *may be*, fifty years later; Thomas Hardy, the poet of to-day, has also sung in lines well worthy, of the *might have been;* but the two songs do not clash.

The many harvests have ripened in turn. "The High Crusades to lessen tears" are following on the harvests; and true teachers, wise, hopeful, and sincere, still hold their own among the brawling empirics of the hour.

Many of the growing convictions of to-day were first pre-echoed in those bygone pages. I remember, long after my father's death, hearing Leslie Stephen, who was then editor, speaking with admiring warmth of some of Ruskin's later writings. But when the series first appeared in the *Cornhill*, so great an outcry was raised, that the papers had to be stopped.

The names are recorded of those who used to meet at the *Cornhill* dinners month after month —honoured, familiar names of people who were then at work, writing papers still read, designing pictures which are not forgotten. When the time came for my father to leave the editorial chair, these meetings went on, and he still joined the good company, only he felt a great relief from the straining and recurrent cares of editorship. It was in March 1862 he wrote to Mr. Smith resigning his post.

"No one can doubt that he came to a wise

decision," writes Mr. George Smith, and he goes on: "I like to think that the tender heart of this noble man of genius was not troubled by editorial thorns during the remainder of his life."

His life did not last very long. At my father's death in 1863 my sister and I were in troubled perplexity about his various copyrights, which were all in various hands and unmanageable for us, and quite unrealisable. Things seemed at a deadlock, when our good friend came forward with a liberal and timely offer beyond anything my father had told us the copyrights were worth. It was then that Messrs. Smith & Elder bought up the various rights and administered the whole, with results which were eventually to benefit all concerned. I like to quote the words written by Leslie Stephen, my brother-in-law, which seem to me to give so vivid an aspect of the founder of the *Cornhill*, and of the *Dictionary of National Biography:* "A good commander must, I take it, be in the first place, a good man of business, and, conversely, Smith's faculty for business would have gone a long way to the making of a leader in war. . . . A man, as

Johnson wisely remarks, can seldom be employed more innocently than in making money, and Smith as a man of business might claim the benefit of that dictum. But he would not have had positive claims upon public gratitude if he had not combined this with loftier aims. . . . It was a pleasure to work with a man so much above petty considerations, and so appreciative (sometimes, perhaps, beyond their merits) of men whose abilities lay in a less practical direction. Smith had the true chivalrous spirit which makes thorough co-operation possible. Thackeray would have been gratified, but not surprised, could it have been revealed to him that after his death his daughters would find his old ally the most helpful and affectionate of friends and advisers."

Now that the *Cornhill* has more than fulfilled its vigorous fiftieth year, it is impossible for those nearly connected with it not to look back with pride at its faithful career. Reading in the memoir by Sir Sidney Lee, in that "in memoriam" from which I have quoted, and still more in the remembrance of life's experience, the words of the Psalmist recur to my mind—

"Using no deceit in his tongue, nor doing evil to his neighbour, swearing to his neighbour and disappointing him not, though it were to his own hindrance." They seem most fitly to speak of such a generous and abiding history.

A MEETING IN A GARDEN

MAY-TIME 1903

The following little paper owes its chief interest to the fact that the Good Samaritans therein mentioned were Canon Barnett and his wife journeying through Surrey, driving in a little carriage, and calling by chance at the Hurst on Hambledon Green, where we were staying in the absence of the hostesses themselves. This was written in May 1903, ten years ago, and we can realise what the humane impulse and practical leadership of these Samaritans has brought about since then. It is good to recall even an hour spent in such company.

Canon Barnett's death is one of those that must affect all who have realised what his noble life was; to those who lived round about him; to others who turned to him with natural impulse, not personally, but with instinctive trust and admiration. No one could ever speak as Mrs. Barnett has spoken in the noble words she has quoted concerning her husband. One of these texts seems written for him. " There is a vision in the heart of each, of justice, mercy, wisdom, tenderness to wrong and pain, and knowledge of its cure."

Some one has told me of Canon Barnett at Darjeeling, reading out Abt Vogler to his wife and his friends as he rested there. Others of us who may not have heard him read, have listened to his fine voice in the Abbey; it still seems speaking; in his life, and his beliefs, and in his teaching in the great Abbey itself, as in the cloister without, or in Whitechapel, where the struggle is so hard, or in the suburbs, where a lesson has been taught and an example of happiness has been set, which will not *cease while men suffer, while poets utter, while generous lives are given to truth.*

For the last three or four days, looking across the village green where many white geese are disporting themselves, in the company of cows tranquilly browsing, we have watched Blackdown and Hindhead, sometimes splendid in blue and purple, sometimes wound in silver mist. Every hour has held its own delight. The very first morning after we came the cuckoo began at four o'clock calling to sluggards to arise, to look out at the sight of the mountain-tops beneath the morning's sovereign eye, at the wide valley with its kindling lights, at the whole space of nature rejoicing and vibrating in the early dawn, with flights of birds and with songs of triumph. The house we are staying in is full of delightful things, and charming possessions of books and pictures, but as yet we have not looked or thought of any of them. This burst of summer has been the one predominant fact in our minds, and the refrain of every thrush and blackbird, the meaning of every leaf and shining blade seems to be an entreaty to beneficent human beings to render grace for all this space and

A MEETING IN A GARDEN

melody, and to prize it for our own joy and for that of others.

While I still lived in London—was it a year or a week ago—I looked at the papers and read with an Englishwoman's complacency of vast sums bestowed in every direction on "improvements," decorations, demolitions; I read of sales by auction, of pictures fetching unimaginable record-prices, of first editions going for hundreds, china pots for thousands; I read of magnificent doings and banquets, of libraries scattered all over the country by benevolent millionaires. But while I read of all these excellent things I did *not* read of provisions by magnificent donors of air and light, and space and peace for those who are in want of them; nor did I read of munificent thousands flowing in for the protection of the beauty of the open spaces which are with us still. Here and there a park is opened (and blessed be the givers thereof), an acre or two is saved, with much trouble and appealing print, from the brick-bats, a disused graveyard is arranged with tasteful iron seats for the use of the living. We are like the king in the fairy tale, we seem more inclined to give our willing largesses to the artificial nightingales than to the real ones. These latter literally, alas, go to the wall. Groves are cut down, singing birds are silenced, the devouring monster of greed and confusion and disorganisation steadily demands his tribute year after year. He is not of the sea, but of the slum; and knight after knight, child after child, maiden after maiden fall beneath his grasping clutch and poisonous breath. Is he not even now crawling up along the beautiful old gardens of Chelsea, doomed one by one to be sacrificed. Even the Paradise of Dante was arranged with regard to open spaces and in circles, but in the comparatively limited areas at our disposal, all seems to be left to chance, to the luck of the moment, to the fancy of the owner.

And this is the gist of what I write, amid that wonder of beauty which is in the world, and which comes home again and again to so many of us as soon as we have a little time to breathe and to admire. A friend to whom I exclaimed yesterday as we stood together in the garden listening to the choirs overhead, sympathised both with my pleasure and my complaint that all this silence and inspiration had its price, could be *bought and sold;* and that even here, in this peaceful land, bricks and villas are not unknown.

My companion, standing among these borders of iris and fragrant pink and delicate campion, handed me not a flower but a (metaphorical) nettle to grasp. "Of course," he said, "every owner of land very naturally objects, just as you do, to seeing villas and small workmen's houses rising against his horizons, and every builder is only too glad to secure open spaces at other people's expense; meanwhile people must have houses to live in, population increases, and we are not yet quite prepared to follow Herod's example. . . ." Grasping my nettle, it occurs to me that to this, one might reply that beauty is an indefinable thing, which depends on proportion, on suitability, on good workmanship (Nature we know gives us the best workmanship possible under every circumstance). Houses must come, but they should be properly built and in proper places, and what we want in our growing towns and villages and country places is not stagnation, nor highly advantageous building speculations, but a liberal economy in the distribution of habitation and space and air, the same care and art as that which is given, for instance, to shipbuilding or to machinery, to ensure the most effectual results with the least waste of space and expense; we do not want a whole country side spoilt by a couple of stray red villas set up where some builder can make most by them. Why should not this art of proportionate distribution, for which I know no name, be applied to the necessities of daily life? Why are there no Supreme Courts for home-beauty and comfort, and economy of ugliness, as well as Treasuries and Foreign Offices? Why are there not councils for the ordaining of necessary amenities as well as for the suppression of those things which have gone hopelessly wrong? I know there are many societies, each wise and delightful in intention, but chiefly the outcome of private feeling; what we need is a Court with wisdom to will and power to decide.

A Good Samaritan and his wife came here on their way not long ago and stopped for an hour to rest in this green corner. To them (and they are Gardeners, indeed, in the best

A MEETING IN A GARDEN

sense of the term), I confess I owe the impulse which now urges me to write this. "I find the longer I live the more I care for open spaces," said the wife. "In all the schemes which are daily started there is hardly ever room enough allowed for space; for birds to fly, for winds to blow, for children to play." And then the other of these Good Samaritans, who had been tying up his pony in a neighbouring shed, now joining into our talk, said, "At this very minute, I know of a beautiful green place with trees marked for building lots, within a twopenny fare of the heart of the City. It could be bought very cheap. Any very rich man could give it to some of the thousand poor ones who are choking for breath and peace and who might come up in the Tube and enjoy themselves. . . . If it is not saved the chance of an open space easily reached and full of pleasure and profit will be gone for ever. This is what working people want even more than books."

And this is what working people owe to Canon and Mrs. Barnett.

UPSTAIRS AND DOWNSTAIRS

I

EACH generation is a natural postscript to that which has gone before, just as one's own succeeding decades take different views, while the story of life tells on. The stairs still lead from the parlour to the kitchen, the maidens still cook, scrub and tidy up, and break the china, and wring the cloths, and sweep away the litter of each succeeding day. The present superintending genius of Mabys still builds her altars, lights her friendly shrines; still befriends the forlorn; still takes girls in hand, holds them up when they are slipping, starts them in life over and over again, nurses them in illness, makes pleasures for them along the way. Mabys was a young and immature personage when the writer first made her acquaintance; she is now an experienced ancient dame with a most enormous family to provide for—those 5851 little orphans who depend upon her so greatly.

When Mrs. Senior was appointed by Mr. Stansfeld inspector of workhouse schools, certain facts became painfully apparent to her. Two-thirds of the girls whose careers were traced were utter failures, and she consulted with one friend, among others, who gave her the result of the experience she had gained in Bristol. Many registers were gone into, and many statements and facts collected. (I remember seeing the kind women absorbed in their work at a big table covered with papers.) Mabys was started on the model of the Bristol enterprise, where the scheme had been worked out under the name of the Preventive Mission. This had been the doing of four ladies—Miss Mary Carpenter, Miss Margaret Elliot, Miss Frances Power Cobbe, and Miss Sarah Stephen. It proved successful, and it spread all over London and was copied in many other places.

Besides the central office in London, there are branch offices everywhere. Each of these offices means a committee and a certain proportion of visitors who undertake to help and care for a number of little girls who from circumstances are among the most absolutely friendless and helpless members of society. Their fathers have abandoned them, or are dead. Their mothers are dead or mad or drunken. They have no relations, or, worse still, only bad ones. They have been kept alive by the State; but the State is at best more of an incubator than a parent, and this association has tried to help the children with some heart, and pity to spare for so much childish misery.

Mabys may be long past her youth, as I have said, but she is full of spirit and energy still. Her votaries are to be counted by thousands. A number of them poured into the great Hall in Pimlico the other day, where the cakes and the tables and stacks of bread and butter were sorted out, and girls of every shape and size were assembling round huge tea-pots in a pleasant camaraderie. As each couple and triplet of girls entered the hall a ministering lady with a pencil and paper met them and pointed out their seats. Some young servants looked trim, some looked smart, others dazed, others were delightful, with charming faces and merry spirits. Of these many had attended year after year. I was shown the *doyennes* of this guild, the experienced who, being over twenty years of age, are no longer eligible to belong to it, but who are associated in the work as "Mabys helpers," and deputed in turn to visit and advise younger and less capable novices in their various kitchens and pantries. After the feast came music and some pretty plays, and then, as happens to us all in turn, the guests had to go back to their work once more and take off their smart hats and ribbons, and tie on their aprons and their little starched caps.

These young guests mainly come from the district schools, though a certain number have struggling homes of their own, from which they apply to Mabys for assistance. Some are foundlings, others are orphans, some have not even this small privilege. In explanation of this cynical sentence, let me quote from a card lately received from one of the maidens, to whom the secretary wrote asking for her mother's or her sister's address. The card, duly dated and labelled, "From Ellen C. *re* Alice C., April '06, B. VI.," arrived at the central office, and goes to the point at once: "Dear Miss,—I am very pleased to tell you I don't know where neither are, if I did know I would tell you, but if we knew where we both were I am afraid I should not be doing as I am."

Whether Alice was ever discovered, and whether Ellen continued to prosper, and whether they went on doing as they did, is all noted and inscribed in the admirably kept books of the society, and I do realise what it must have been to Ellen ill or in difficulties, and in the absence of any desirable natural protector, to have a "Dear Miss" to consult with.

II

The first office of the Association ever opened was at Chelsea. It is a friendly little place, which takes a benevolent interest in the various domestic fortunes and misfortunes of the neighbourhood. If you go there of a Monday morning you may find a room full of customers of various sizes, and an almost providential adjustment of different requirements.

"Well, you see," a stout lady was saying confidentially, "I'm so much alone of evenings, my husband being out with the carriage, I want a girl for comp'ny as much as anything else. I don't want no housework from her. I want her to do any little odd jobs I can't attend to myself, and to mind the children. That was a good little girl enough you sent me, Miss Y——; but dear me, she was always a-crying for her mother. I let her out on Mondays, and Wednesdays, and Fridays; but she wanted to go home at night as well, and now she says she won't stay."

"It's her first place, ma'am," says Miss Y——. "They are apt to be home-sick at first; but here is a very good little girl who has no home, poor child. Fanny, my dear, should you like to live with Mrs. —— and take care of her nice little children? You might like to take her back with you now directly, ma'am, and show her the place and the dear children?"

Smiling Fanny steps forward briskly, and off they go together. Then a pretty young lady, fashionably dressed in a fur tippet, begins:

"That girl was no good at all, Miss Y——. Such a dance as she led me! She came and gave me a reference miles away, and ill as I was I dragged myself there; and when I got to the house she herself opened the door, and said her mistress was out and was never at home at all. I said at once, 'You don't want to come to us, and you haven't the courage to say so,' and then she shut the door in my face and ran away! The fact is, many don't like houses with apartments. Our first floor is vacant at present, but I hope it will soon be let; and I should be so glad to find a girl who would come at once, and who knows something of cookery, though my mother always likes to superintend herself in the kitchen."

"There is a young woman here who says she can cook," says the superintendent doubtfully, "but there seems to be some difficulty about getting her character. Do you think we had better write to your mistress for it, my dear?"

A fierce, wild beast-looking creature, who had been glaring in a corner, here in answer growls, "I don't know, I'm sure."

"Why did you leave?" says the young lady.

"'Cos she had such a wiolent temper," says the girl, looking more and more ferocious.

"That is a sad thing for anybody to have," said the young lady gravely.

At this moment a boy puts his head in at the door. "Got any work for me?" says he.

"No, no," cry all the girls together. "This isn't for boys; this is for females," and the head disappears.

"Well, and what do you want?" says the superintendent, quite bright and interested with each case as it turns up, and a spruce young person, who had been listening attentively, steps forward and says, looking hard at the young lady in the tippet:

"I wish for a place, if you please, ma'am, with a little cooking in it, where the lady herself superingtends in the kitchen—a ladies' house that lets apartments, if you please; and I shouldn't wish for a private house, only an apartment house." At which the young mistress, much pleased, steps forward, and a private confabulation immediately begins.

While these two people are settling their affairs a mysterious person in a veil enters, and asks anxiously in a sort of whisper, "Have you heard of anything for me, Miss? You see (emphatically) it is something so *very* particular that I require, quite out of the common."

"Just so," says Miss Y——. "I won't forget."

"Don't forget, and you won't mention the circumstances to any one," says the other, and exit mysteriously with a confidential sign.

Follows a smiling little creature, with large round eyes.

"Well," said Miss Y——, who is certainly untiring in sympathy and kindness, "is it all right? Are you engaged, Polly?"

"Please, Miss, I'm *much* too short," says the little maiden.

As we have said, it is not only the district girls who apply at these offices; all the young persons of the neighbourhood are made welcome by the recording angels (so they seem to me), who remember their names, invite them to take a seat on the bench, produce big books with their histories, necessities, and qualifications all written down, and by the help of which they are more or less "suited." Besides a mistress, a kitchen to scrub, if they behave themselves they are also presented with a badge and honourable decoration, fastened by a blue ribbon, and eventually they are promoted to a red ribbon, the high badge of honour for these young warriors. And though some people may smile, it is, when we come to think of it, a hardly earned distinction, well deserved as any soldier's cross. What a campaign for them—a daily fight with the powers of darkness and ignorance, with dust, with dirt, with disorder. Where should we be without our little serving girls? At this moment, as I write by a comfortable fire, I hear the sound of a virtuous and matutinal broom in the cold passages below, and I reflect that these 8000 little beings on the books are hard at work all over London and fighting chaos in the foggy twilight of a winter's morning.

It is a hard life at best for some of them; so hard that they break down utterly in the struggle with temper and other tempers, with inexperience, with temptations of every sort. If one thinks of it one can imagine it all, and the impatience, and the petty deceptions, and the childish longings, almost irresistible, one might think, to little waifs who have no one to look to for praise if they are good, or for blame if they are naughty. And yet, indeed, they are not ungrateful; they respond to any word of real friendship. "I am quite frightened sometimes to find how much they think of my opinion," said a good friend the other day, who has for some years past worked steadily for the Association. "They make me quite ashamed when they produce my wretched little notes out of their pockets." When I asked this lady about the children's comparative friendlessness, she said it was very rare to find them absolutely alone, but that, in truth, friends are often far worse enemies than loneliness. They come and grasp at their poor little earnings. They lead them into mischief out of wanton wickedness, and desert them in their troubles. A girl came staggering into her office not long ago, so ill that she could hardly stand. She had gone to her sister, whom she had always helped with her wages, and lain in bed two days with fever, and then her sister would not let her stay, and turned her into the street, though she fell twice as she was dressing. It was a case of smallpox, and the poor thing was sent off to the Smallpox Hospital. "I went to see her there," said Miss T——, speaking quite as a matter of course. "The poor child began searching under her pillow and showed me a little scrap of a note I had written her a year before, which she had carried about ever since. One can scarcely believe," the kind lady said, "how they prize a little interest, a little friendly intercourse with some one who cares about what happens to them."

IN MY LADY'S CHAMBER

I

THEY were sitting by the fire one evening about Easter time, two women, to whom the gloaming hours made little difference, except that the lady of the house poked the comfortable embers and shut the French windows of the room, which had been open to a twilight garden, where narcissus and blue scilla were springing and fruit trees were coming into blossom, and whence the echoes of Cambridge clocks and chimes reached now and again, borne across wide open flats. The two ladies, meeting after a long interval, sat talking over the time which had passed, comparing the various scraps of interest, of divination of feeling, which belonged in common to them both.

One of them, who had arrived that day, brought with her a varied but somewhat tangled tune, echoes of work, of diversion, of perplexity. The home-keeping friend's light seemed to play on each of these in turn, putting new meaning and interpretations, to which her visitor could only respond gratefully and not without admiration. All the remembrance of things past seemed to awaken that evening and to come back into existence more vividly every moment as the two, so familiar in long-tried affection—in agreement and in divergence also—held their peaceful session; almost unconsciously counting up the thens and the nows, the things they cared for and those they had hoped for, and the failures, as well as the facts of success they both liked to dwell upon with that sort of surprise which is even greater, perhaps, in success than that which any sense of failure brings with it. And as they recalled efforts which had succeeded, the lives which to the end had ever kept to their high level, counting up the treasure-trove, which belongs to us all indeed, it happened that in their talk they came to the mention of one name among others—that of Mrs. Nassau Senior —and of the Association which will ever be linked with her memory.

Mrs. Senior's name will always be associated with that of Mabys, of which she was indeed the founder, feeling as she did the want of some such help for girls coming out of workhouse schools and asylums, friendless and homeless, leaving the shelter and limitations in which they had been brought up for the world, where rules are not, nor safeguards, and the results were often disastrous, as they still are at times.

The old friends looked at each other with a common feeling of pleasure in that one woman's achievements, and in the charm of a personality still present after a quarter of a century. What follows is but a record of an evening's talk.

II

We could almost believe now and again as we look at pictures which we have known always that mysterious things have happened to them since we saw them first—that new expressions have come into them. Was Turner's "Evening Star," for instance, as brightly scintillating as now when the painter first moved away from his canvas, or has the silver ocean, travelling out of space, come into the picture since it was first painted? It is not so with some lives we have loved and admired. The light seems to come into them.

Many of us may have this impression looking at Watts's fine portrait of Mrs. Nassau Senior, so familiar to the two interlocutors quoted above. It was once a beautiful picture and a most charming likeness, but now it seems something more. The painter had the spirit of divination, and it was as if he foresaw and remembered, too, while he stood painting at his easel. In this particular picture he has not only given us an actual portrait, but he has painted an abiding presence, the history of a life. The lady kneels to reach the flowers; her absorbed and careful looks are fixed upon the lilies which she is watering; one fair hand rests upon the marble table, the other with rosy-tipped fingers holds up the glass bowl brimming with water. Her violet dress—how well it always became her—hangs in straight folds from her waist; her beautiful flood of yellow hair flows in ripples. Everything in the painting is warm in tone; it is all simple, yet gorgeous; so is the ancient Indian shawl of orange and blue and scarlet, so is the big chair which is covered with Turkey twill; the green walls are only papered with ordinary hangings; but the various colours vibrate round the sweet head, which is bending with exquisite concern and intentness, and which is the soul of it all. A tray of hothouse flowers stands waiting on the floor. There are sprays of azalea and crown-imperials, and geraniums and maiden-hair ferns; but the lady has left them to water the growing lilies, and the feeling of peaceful ministry and the warmth of generous existence, all are somehow told in the picture, as it was in the life itself, which ended so long ago, which is so beneficent still.

Watts himself has written of this picture, of the intention he had when he created it, making her, as he says, "water a flowering root with so much solicitude"; and he goes on to dwell upon "the aspirations and affections which are sometimes with difficulty kept alive in the crush of artificial society. I love," he writes in a letter to her, "to think of you cultivating these rare roots. . . . No, not rare:

"' By God's dear grace not rare;
In many a lonely homestead blooming strong.'"

. . . As I quote from Watts's letter I cannot help also remembering a saying of Ruskin, in which he, too, dwells on a woman's vocation. "A true lady," Ruskin says, "should be a princess, a washerwoman—yes, a washerwoman, to wash with water, to cleanse, to purify wherever she goes, to set disordered things in orderly array. . . . This is a woman's mission."

III

Some of us may still remember Elm House, where the Seniors lived at Wandsworth, and the long, low drawing-room, with its big bow-window opening to a garden full of gay parterres, where lawns ran to the distant boundary, while beyond again lay a far-away horizon. It was not the sea that one saw spreading before one's eyes, but the vast plateau of London, with its drifting vapours and its ripple of housetops flowing to meet the sky-line. The room itself was pleasant, sunny, and well-worn. There were old rugs spread on the stained floors (they were not as yet in fashion as they are now); many pictures were hanging on the walls; a varied gallery, good and indifferent; among the good were one or two of Watts's finest portraits, and I can also remember a Madonna's head with a heavy blue veil, and in juxtaposition a Pompeian sort of ballet girl, almost springing from the frame; and then, besides the pictures, there was a sense of music in the air, and of flowers, and of more flowers. The long piano was piled with music-books. Mrs. Nassau Senior, the mistress of the house, used to play her own chords and accompany herself as she poured out her full heart in strains beautiful and measured rather than profuse.

Garcia had been Mrs. Senior's singing master, and he would sometimes be present among the rest. I heard him speaking of her with affectionate admiration when he was a hundred years old, in his honourable age. How clear was her voice, how it rang and vibrated! For those who loved to listen to it, her "Vado ben spesso" rings on still. The true notes flowed; she did not seem to make any effort. She would cease singing to make some old friend welcome, and take to her music again as a matter of course. There was no solemnity in her performance, and yet I have heard Mrs. Sartoris[1] say that it was

---

[1] Mrs. Sartoris—Adelaide Kemble—has given a charming account of Mrs. Senior in her *Reflections of Joseph Heywood*, under the name of "Christian Rupert."

because of the unremitting work of years, and because of Mrs. Senior's devotion to her art with absolute and conscientious determination, that she could use her voice as she did with tender and brilliant ease. It was a good sword indeed to defend the right. I heard a pretty story of a room full of Whitechapel boys and girls in revolt, and suddenly, when the clamour was at its height, she stood up quietly and began to sing, and the storm stopped and the room became silent and attentive. Sir Theodore Martin told me that he had only met Mrs. Senior once, one day when she was singing an Irish ballad to George Eliot at North Bank, "Far from the land where her young hero sleeps," which was written of Emmet. Sir Theodore said that forty years after he "could hear the notes still quite plainly." Some voices have this peculiar quality of vibrating on and on.

Stately and charming people used to assemble at Elm House. It is an old saying that people of a certain stamp attract each other. It was a really remarkable assemblage of accomplished and beautiful women who were in the habit of coming there, that home so bare, so simple, and yet so luxurious. It was like a foreign colony. The old roof held father, mother, son, the two widowed grandmothers—each in her own rooms, with her own attendant and the consequent vibrations. There was a younger brother [1] also, with his flock of motherless children. The servants were like friends, not servants.

There is a letter with a date to it, February 1874, written by Mrs. Senior from a little cottage in the Isle of Wight which Mrs. Cameron had lately altered and devised, and which has belonged to the writer at intervals for years. That one winter Mrs. Senior went there to stay in it. Her son has let me see the letter, which begins with a motherly blessing, then continues:

"My dear, this is the Porch, the gate of Heaven. There is a sense of repose that I think one must feel just after death before beginning the new life. It is inconceivable how I enjoy it. I do nothing for hours together. The sitting-room opens into a tiny conservatory, and through the open window one hears the enchanted moan

---

[1] H. H., now gone to his rest, after making a new home in a new world.

THE PORCH

of the sea and the song of the birds. We are a long way from the sea, but I hear it; I wake at six and hear the earliest pipe of half-awakened birds, and I go to sleep with the sea in my ears and a lovely star looking in at my window. . . . We are to lunch at the Prinseps' to-morrow, as I want to see Watts. He is going to London to paint portraits. His house is perfectly charming. I am dying to build a house. It has rained all this morning, and we could not go to church; now it seems clearing, and the sun thinks of shining . . . a constant thanksgiving and prayer goes up from my heart as I rest and am thankful."

What a grace is rest to those who work without ceasing!

There is a description of an evening at Farringford and of the mysterious walk there—the veiled stars and the dark garden with its great shrubs and the great room and the poet within, reading, and Lady Tennyson, like St. Monica, lying on her couch. All this was but a short break in the constant unending work of Jeanie Senior's life, in her gallant fight with suffering. During the first week of this holiday she could not forget, she could not rest, but after her three weeks she writes to her son: "I feel perfectly up to my work now, and have fits of longing to be at *Paupers* again, though in general I am absorbed by the delight of the beauty of everything, and the desire to pass the remaining years of my life in painting scenes in the Isle of Wight! . . ."

She describes a visit she paid with Mr. Watts to a cottage her mother, Mrs. Hughes, eventually bought:

"The garden was most sunny and warm, and the view of the heath and the sea really lovely. There was a high north wind, and the colour of the sea light green and purple, with splendid white tops to the waves. The bit of heath, too, is lovely, but there is no field for a cow, which would be a drawback in mother's eyes."

Some other painter should have been there to paint the two figures looking across the gorse common at the white crests of the waves. Watts with his serene and stately looks, the lady, who had but such a little while to live, but who to the last tried for practical beauty in life as far as in her lay, and happiness and deliverance from evil for others. And among all her good practical works the Metropolitan Association for Befriending Young Servants has been one to last and to spread its useful harvest under the care of those who have come after her. Mabys perhaps sprang from the foam of those waves that day as they broke upon Colwell Bay.

THE END